MW01005256

The Hardest Part About

A Ten-Year Journey through Grief

Sawyer Small

WestBow Press books may be ordered through booksellers or by contacting:

WestBow Press
A Division of Thomas Nelson & Zondervan
1663 Liberty Drive
Bloomington, IN 47403
www.westbowpress.com
1 (866) 928-1240

ISBN: 978-1-9736-4261-9 (sc)
ISBN: 978-1-9736-4260-2 (hc)
ISBN: 978-1-9736-4262-6 (e)

Library of Congress Control Number: 2018912186

Print information available on the last page.

WestBow Press rev. date: 10/25/2018

For Rebecca J. Small—the mother, daughter, sister, aunt, godmother, friend, and mentor to many. You continue to teach us more about life even after your death.

and

For my family and friends who walked beside me and with one another throughout the journey. Your voices were heard in the writing of this book. Your grief is heard.

Contents

Introduction

One of the hardest things about books on grief is knowing how to start to help keep it brief. I'm stuck inside my head trying to break it into parts, remembering the lessons that the grief imparts. In a complex world, wanting to find our way out, we begin with four words: **the hardest part about.**

Four simple words. Such a small amount of words expressed by a friend, spouse, family member, coworker, and so on can go in many different directions. You may find that there are times when you are starting a sentence with these four words with the intent of delving into your own feelings or as a way to express the perceived pain of a situation so that others may understand where your mind and heart were at in that moment. You may also be thinking about these four words as you reflect on the fact you picked up a book that's centered on grief. Regardless, hearing or saying the phrase "the hardest part about" means that a story is about to be told.

To anyone, it's easy to find the negative in our lives and the need to express our anger, powerlessness, frustrations, or misfortunes to others in hopes that we may feel better about our situations. Possibly, we just want to receive the sympathy of our friends or family to comfort us. Growing up, we often find anything that's the slightest bit negative in our lives in order to express our voices and be a part of the culture of hurting and suffering individuals. From middle school and high schoolers expressing their failures in life over broken relationships, to college students struggling to find meaning in their future lives, and to adults not satisfied with their work environment—we all find a use for the phrase "the hardest part about."

Then again, maybe our use of these words is to help us define our periods of self-improvement and the times in our lives that we felt uncomfortable. This view means that we have been able to look back on the past. We have been able to define what we were feeling and what we actually learned from the situation—almost as afterthoughts. I like to take this view, personally, because when you are in the midst of the fray, the words don't always come naturally. You may be frozen or numb to what you are actually feeling and only able to express the surface level aspects of the grief that you can currently see or feel. Research has even shown that your brain's area for expressive speech, Broca's area, can decrease in activity when you try to reexperience or relive trauma.[1] You are truly at a loss for words.

As you continue to come out of the fray and you watch your story continue to unfold, you are able to look back on the previous chapters and see how you got to your current one. Now is when you are able to ask the important questions of where each chapter started, who was there, who was helping to tell the story, and where you were at physically, emotionally, spiritually, and so on. You start to see the bigger picture and realize how the experience has influenced many aspects in your own story (e.g., what has changed in importance and how do I define myself now).

The story that follows is my own personal ten-year journey through grief, an afterthought of my own "misfortunes." After losing a mother at the young age of fourteen, the primary focus of my journey has been learning to live with the changes that inevitably occurred. As Anne Roiphe wrote, "Grief is in two parts. The first is loss. The second is the remaking of life."[2] Thus, my grief journey does not end after I retell my mom's diagnosis, treatment, and death. My life continued on, and I had to do what more than 1.9 million other children in America today have to do—learn to accept the death of a parent.[3]

As my mom's ten-year anniversary approached—April 10, 2018—I needed to take the time to reflect on the roller-coaster ride these years have been. My daily work as a music therapist in a mental and behavioral health facility has provided me with humbling moments that are reminders I need to address my own grief as well. How did I resolve the many facets of grief that I work on with my clients? Am I empathizing with their stories more because I see bits of those stories within my own? I believe that sometimes I do, but I also believe that I've been able to avoid disclosing my own personal experiences in order to keep a professional relationship—as my many mentors have taught me to do. However, this does not stop clients from being intrigued as to why I choose to lead a grief-and-loss therapy group every week, and I have to stop and think when I notice my clients also using the phrase "the hardest part about."

In the world of grief, that phrase can go many different ways: "The hardest part about saying my last goodbye was ..." or "The hardest part about the funeral was ..." Grief is not limited to just death, though. We experience grief through losses such as the loss of employment, graduating school and leaving home, a diagnosis of dementia or other life-deteriorating illnesses, loss of security and control over a situation, loss of a friendship or familial relationship due to estrangement, a miscarriage, loss of a childhood dream, retirement, and so on.[4] The list is extensive—some even included in this story—but each loss triggers different emotions and reactions. Those reactions vary from person to person and are expressed in a variety of ways—even within the same individual.

No matter what book or resource you read, you will be reminded that everyone has their own way of grieving and that whatever way you grieve is right for you. You can analyze how you handled your grief, asking yourself, "Why can't I cry?" or "Why didn't I react like my brother, sister, aunt, uncle, or someone else did to the loss that we all shared?" You have to accept that the way you grieved is exactly that. There are no prescribed steps to properly follow. There is no specific time frame for grieving as well because there are many factors that contribute to the intensity of the loss, such as your relationship with that person or thing, whether the loss was sudden or if you had the chance to anticipate (was there a proper goodbye?), and your ability to deal with the stressors both emotionally and psychologically.[5]

The early days of my grief are summed up perfectly by Lonestar: "Not a day goes by that I don't think of you."[6] Although I had accepted my mom's death, allowing me to move on in a socially acceptable way, my grief was still there. I lived each day expecting to *live through* the emotions of that day. My reactions to the loss would simply pop up again from time to time in my life. She was on my mind through many of my decisions, and through further experiences with loss, I was brought back to remembering all of the unresolved sensitivity that I had. I often worried about my future, going further into a trench of anxiety when I remembered she wasn't going to be a part of those future milestones. At the same time, there are many memories that I share in this book that have provided periods of encouragement when I thought of her.

The memories I chose to include in this book are very vivid in my mind. I remember thinking during these events that although I would forget some of the precise dialogue and details, I would still remember the essence of these moments. I knew at these times that they were unique. They were forever etched in the long-term, explicit memory of my brain, an area which is influenced by the emotional processor—the amygdala.[7] To also put in perspective, I was experiencing many of these events as a young mind, and I wrote these words in a way that highlights where my thinking was at in those years. Adolescents, and especially children, have more neural plasticity than adults. Research demonstrates that another area of memory in our brains, the hippocampus, has an "unusual capacity" for regeneration and neural plasticity.[8] Therefore, my memories were being adapted in the face of stress, possibly aiding and expediting my path of learning resilience for future stressful events.

Each chapter follows my journey of learning this resilience, starting with a different "hardest-part-about" aspect of grief. In my own story, I discuss the early shock of my mom's diagnosis, the following anticipation of her death, the search for meaning, realization of change, and the further repackaging of this layered and cyclical grief journey. I would be remiss if I claimed to be the only character affected by the different varieties of grief and loss in this story, though. The other real-life characters included in my story also lost a mother, a sister, a wife, a daughter, an aunt, and a friend. They each have their own stories, interwoven into my own, that I felt were important to include in this discussion on how grief, specifically bereavement, is handled in different ways.

These "perspective chapters" are included in between my own—written in the words of my family and the friends of my mother. The chapters describe what they view "the hardest part about" was, regarding their relationships with my mother. As you read specific events that were significant in my own memory, you then may find yourself reading another point of view that has allowed the story to be expanded and influenced from a different mind. Through Frederic Bartlett's studies, we learn that memories are influenced by different life views and by the perceptions we have of an event, which both cause the memories to change over time depending on those perceptions.[9] Upon asking my family and the friends of my mother to write their own stories, I recognized that some of their memories could have changed in these past ten years just as mine did. Regardless, I felt that reading what they *still* remembered would help myself and you—the reader—to understand the lasting effects and impact that different perceptions can have on the memory of grief.

I also delve into discussion about coping mechanisms throughout the entire story. I may not have known the definition of "coping" or understood what I was doing had its own course of study in psychology as a teenager, but nevertheless, I developed many of my own. I speak numerously about the impact music had in my life, ultimately leading me to pursue my current career as a music therapist, a profession that has thankfully been receiving more recognition in the past few decades and has allowed me to advocate for the efficacy of music on emotional regulation. You will read the origins of my affinity for music, which then became a major theme throughout my grief journey.

However, I, and various other family members of mine, also reference our faiths or spiritualities as lasting coping skills. I wanted to write this book in a way that showcased what we believed was our way of dealing with the death of a loved one. My hope is that any reader who views him- or herself as religious, spiritual, both, or neither, can still find comforting words in this story—even within its Christian context. Whether you rely on sacred scripture or simply a positive phrase or mantra, the use of comforting words is a way of coping that's made personal to each individual.

Grief has luckily been studied more frequently in the past

century. Starting with publications on death and dying, such as John Hinton's book, *Dying*, in 1967[10] and Elisabeth Kubler-Ross's many publications from 1960–2000, the analysis of the other areas of grief and trauma has been researched both psychologically and neurologically since then. I didn't intend for this book to be a source of compiled research because it's first and foremost a grief *story*. However, I chose to use references from various publications in hopes that they may spark curiosity for the expansive literature that's already out there, as well as to give the support readers may need beyond the words I've compiled.

"The hardest part about" is just the beginning to the words that are composed in each chapter, but these four words continue to be present throughout how my family and I view our grief. In the context of losing a loved one, this phrase is able to begin to communicate the expansive package of emotions that come with this type of experience. The most interesting and important thing to realize is that even though the sentences may start the same, they are taken in many different ways, depending on the person writing and their situation. For this reason, as you read these four words, are you finding yourself telling a similar story? Or are you listening to someone else, possibly providing you with insight into an entirely different perspective you'd never before thought to ask about? Do you find yourself interwoven within the various stories?

Stories normally demand a plot, an order, and a linear path, but as Ann Hood stated: "Grief doesn't have a plot. It isn't smooth. There is no beginning and middle and end."[11] In my attempt to write this ten-year journey, I would have to agree with her. I can't pinpoint with accuracy where each literary mark lands and certainly can't see a true ending to all grief in my life. However, like many other things in our lives, it's best to let the story unfold itself.

1 Newly Diagnosed Teenager

The hardest part about the initial grief is the growing sense of uncertainty throughout the unfolding story.

I was only thirteen when my mother learned that she had cancer. It was on my birthday that I could sense that she wasn't feeling well as she kept telling me, "I'm so sorry for ruining your birthday." The tears in her eyes and look of defeat were telling signs that she was upset with herself. Being the anxious person and caring mother that she was, she only wanted the best for me, and that only made her feel worse that she wasn't feeling like her usual perky personality on my special day.

As a forty-two-year-old wife and mother of three at the time, Becki was a personality that you wouldn't forget. Her smile, eyes, and humor shined brightly among anyone she was with, but especially in the presence of children. She worked as a paraprofessional in our town's school system, primarily providing care for elementary students in special education. Whether it was her schoolkids or her actual children, her empathic persona was set on providing the best care and emotional support that she could give. If she could have, she'd have taken from you all the pain or emotional hurting so you wouldn't have to experience any discomfort.

As she began feeling sick during that winter, I noticed a marked difference in her demeanor. I was used to seeing her constant smile and hearing her devilish laugh as she pulled one of her pranks. That birthday, the picture I still hold in my mind is of a defeated individual, tearful on the couch and white as a ghost. We learned at that time that she was anemic, which made her feel physically weak and lightheaded. Her skin looked paler than usual—which was saying much for a natural redhead.

Through this experience, my thirteen-year-old self was learning valuable medical knowledge firsthand. I learned that anemia meant my mom wasn't getting enough red blood cells, which carried oxygen throughout her body. There are many types of anemia that are caused by different things, such as a hereditary defect, chronic diseases, vitamin deficiency, and iron deficiency, as well as a few more causes.[1] Luckily, we learned the cause of my mom's anemia—she was iron deficient.

I may have been a middle-school-level science nerd, but if it was iron my mom needed in her diet, wouldn't giving her more iron be the answer? I remembered seeing pills in our cupboards that were supposed to be iron supplements, so what were we waiting for? Take a couple, and this could all be fixed! Make me a doctor already.

Obviously, the problem was rooted much deeper than a simple iron deficiency. The doctors wanted to run a couple of tests to rule out the possibility of cancer. My mom soon underwent a colonoscopy—a process I knew nothing about until my mom vaguely explained what she'd had to experience. To this day, all I can think about when I hear the word *colonoscopy* is the two Ts: a tube and a TV.

I still remember the day that my mom walked upstairs to my sisters' and my rooms, and through tears, she confirmed the news we didn't want to hear. We had all been hoping that the doctors would say the lump they had found in her colon was just a polyp. At least with a polyp, the doctors would have been able to treat the lump within a couple of months. As for cancer, the diagnosis was unclear.

That day is still so vivid to me because I remember where I was, who was present, and the fact that I was playing *Guitar Hero* on my Xbox when my mom slowly made her way up the stairs. I remember pausing my game in order to go hug her. I will never forget that special moment of embracing my mom along with both of my sisters as we tried our best to comfort her. I believe at that time only she knew the extent of the situation and how the disease would affect her. I also believe that, at this exact time, my grief journey began.

At thirteen years old, I had not had any true experiences of grief. My dad's mother had passed away shortly after I'd been born. She had been battling a brain tumor while my mom was pregnant with me, and my grandmother had been in the hospital from my birth until her death four months later on April 10. Although she was able to see her last grandchild before she passed, I never got to know her other than through keeping a single photo that showed my baby self lying on her chest in the hospital. My mom enjoyed telling me the story of how she and my dad had been leaving the hospital after visiting my grandmother before I was born, and my grandmother had simply said, "Take care of my little boy." Seeing as my mom kept my gender a complete secret from most people, this story had always given me chills.

My only other similar experience with grief was when my

mom's father had a stroke around my twelfth birthday. Even though he thankfully survived the experience, I don't believe I fully understood how serious the situation was. Once again, I just remember playing my video games in the hospital while my mom's family anticipated the possibility of losing him. So, as my mom faced her own uncertainty with cancer, I was facing new emotions that I couldn't even name at the time.

The next year would bring even more uncertainty to my family. My mother started her treatment of both chemotherapy and radiation, which caused her to miss many days of work. One of my sisters, Sydney, was entering her senior year of high school and working toward figuring out where she wanted to go to college. My oldest sister, Mallory, was already in college about two and a half hours away from our hometown. I can only imagine what it was like for her to be so far away from our family in the whirlwind days of my mom's treatment.

I was fortunate enough that as I was entering the eighth grade, my mother was placed with a student who was also in middle school, allowing me to be close to her again. It had been five years since we were both in the same school building. When she was able to work, I could expect her bright smile and soft, caring eyes as we passed in the hall. Sometimes, especially when I was around girls, I could expect her to give a whistle my way or say something that would embarrass me. That woman knew how to make a fool of herself and wasn't afraid to use it as a weapon! Looking back, I now think that her humor and personality made it harder for anyone, including myself, to realize how much the disease was taking from her.

As the treatment continued, however, I was seeing my mother less and less within the halls of school; the disease had spread and was starting to show itself. When I got home, she was either lying on the couch or in her bedroom, looking exhausted. Her newly obtained colostomy bag made her feel ashamed to be seen by anyone other than her family. I wasn't entirely sure why she even had that bag, but I knew I hated it as well for taking away my mom's sanity. I hated the smell. And I hated the bag's entire existence.

Our family dog, Pyper, would always be by her side and follow her wherever she went. Pyper always seemed to be able to comfort all of us, but I always knew that my mom and that dog had a special bond. When we lost our family cat of eleven years earlier that year, we decided to look for a dog. The moment we saw and held Pyper, a Cavalier King Charles cocker spaniel, we knew she was the right one for us. She instantly became our comforter and brought a little bit of happiness back to our family. We sure needed it.

We also needed the community support we were receiving. Throughout my mom's treatment, we always had family friends bringing over dishes of food and meals for our entire family. I know this made my mom feel worse about her condition, knowing that she couldn't pay them back for the generosity she was receiving. Considering this was a woman who ripped up your check right in front of you if you tried to pay her back, I knew this was a difficult subject for her. She was used to giving, not receiving.

My advice to anyone who knows a friend, family member, or colleague going through a rough period is don't hesitate to show your generosity. Despite my mom's reluctance to accept the food offered to us, one of the few positive memories I have of her decline came through a shared meal. We sat together on our couch and ate some of our favorite comfort food—bacon-wrapped shrimp and garlic mashed potatoes from a local restaurant. In that moment, we were simply a mother and son enjoying each other's presence, a moment provided by a friend's generosity.

Nevertheless, as I began to see my mom in her exhausted

state more often, I began to think, Where has my mom gone? Her abrupt change scared me at times, but I avoided any thought of the future of the disease. Looking back, I understand that I was most likely avoiding my emotions as a defense mechanism. But being able to keep track of your own emotions is pretty much impossible as a newly diagnosed teenager.

I remained optimistic, though. I can't help but deny that I was also blessed, or possibly cursed, with the positive outlook that my mother always had—a positive outlook that can be infectious and remain hopeful in spite of any difficult situation.

* * *

I remember going to at least one of my mother's chemo appointments. The room on the hospital unit felt so small, and the lights were so bright. Not to mention, the walls were bland. Did the hospital want their patients to remain depressed?

I spent most of my time watching the television as she received her chemo through the IV pole, and as I recall, she didn't want to talk that much. I was confused and a little offended about this at the time, but I realize now, as I exhibit the same behavior, that my mother and I shared the need to shut down when we are hurting. Words and conversation seem counterproductive when we are mentally, emotionally, and possibly physically, hurting. If we're not in the right mind-set to console ourselves or make sense of our own emotions, then we'd rather hold off on expressing those emotions until our mental fight has de-escalated. For as crazy as that strategy sounds, I've used it many times to alleviate my anxiety; sometimes it seems to work, while other times it inevitably backfires.

After my brief experience with chemo treatments, I don't remember going back with her to another appointment. One was enough for me. I preferred to avoid any thought of the future of her disease. Plus, I was living life as an eighth grader, the top of the middle school food chain. I was enjoying being with friends, being able to take many opportunities to learn more in music activities, and overall, trying to be a typical middle school student.

However, "far from typical" would have been more of an accurate movie title for my spring semester. As my mom missed more days in school, I found myself hanging out with friends more often. I believe my mom wanted me to have as much fun as I could and to not be around her while she was feeling sick. I believe she was also hesitant about me bringing friends over and would have rather had me go to my friends' houses. As my mom was the person I shared everything with, I felt that as I continued to distance myself from her, I was keeping all of my emotions in. My anxious thoughts had nowhere to go, remaining with me until the day that they would be tested.

That day finally came at school when I was in choir class and the intercom gave a familiar tone. *Beep:* "Mrs. Swenson, Sawyer has a phone call in the office."

I looked around, and everyone was staring at me. I looked at my choir teacher, who gave me the nod, and I left through the door. My heart was pounding as I wondered what could have happened to my mom in the past couple of hours since I'd seen her? Also, why did it have to be the choir room, the farthest class I had from the middle school office?

I kept looking up to the ceiling and catching each light as I passed underneath it. Each light felt like my classmates' eyes as they tried to pick up on my reaction to the intercom announcement. The hallway was a straight shot to the middle school portion of the building. I could see the office in sight, but I remember blocking out any people or classrooms around me as I continued to walk. The walk seemed surprisingly fast, possibly due to the increase in my cadence as my thoughts kept racing.

As I finally got to the office, the receptionist looked at me and pointed to the phone that was off the hook on the desk. I walked around the counter, and with my hand shaking, I picked up the phone. I took a deep breath and answered, "Hello?"

I heard a soft, familiar voice, and I was instantly relieved. My mom. "Sawyer," she said, "Grandpa Small died this morning." Her voice seemed a little faint as she was telling me the rest. "Your uncles found him this morning. He had been having breathing problems for some time, and with his old age, they believe this was going to happen at some point. I thought I should let you know."

I truthfully don't remember what I responded to her because I was just relieved to hear her voice. I hung up the phone and walked out of the office. As I walked back to the choir room, my relief faded, and I had the realization that my grandpa had just died. I began thinking, What does this mean? Should I be crying or trying to find my sister in the high school? I don't know what people do in these situations. In fact, I didn't know what grief looked like because I was always hidden away in my video games when others were experiencing theirs. Hollywood movies were the extent of my grief knowledge.

Now I'm expected to walk back into choir, knowing my grandpa died. Can I show emotion? No, I thought, shaking my head, because everyone is already going to be staring at me, wondering about mom. Any emotion will make them think something happened. Give a poker face and just sing, Sawyer. Thank God, it's Friday tomorrow!

2 A Gut Feeling

The hardest part about anticipatory grief is the undercurrent of ambivalence that affects your actions.

Anticipation builds. Like any well-written movie or artistically crafted musical composition, there is a continuation to the climax. The uneasiness builds in the character's development while the orchestra score increases its usage of unwarranted dissonance, all to build the suspense. The movie-goer is taking in each unexpected turn in the unfolding story, experiencing a gut-wrenching feeling in his or her stomach that helps to soften the blow.

Grief also builds. From the initial shock of a diagnosis, or the first experience with a physical loss, your mind begins to wonder, Have I hit my climax already, or is that yet to come? You question where your story is headed and if or when it will lead to a reasonable resolution. These thoughts only lead to more anticipation, giving you that uneasy gut feeling.

In defense, the anticipatory grief then becomes your shield, warning of what you fear might still be in store.

When I made my walk to the middle school office for my phone call, my mind was focused solely on my mom. I had an uneasy feeling and immediate knowledge that the phone call was going to be unsettling, despite who was calling. This gut feeling was trying to tell me that I needed to prepare myself; otherwise, I would be blindsided by grief. But I ignored its warning. Hearing my mom's voice on the other end of the call instantly relieved that feeling, leaving me defenseless to the news that she had to share with me. My reaction was numbness and the perception that I needed to be emotionless as I returned to my classmates.

I reentered the chorus room exactly as I'd expected it to be—with prying eyes. Or at least I just *thought* everyone was staring at me. Part of me wanted people to ask me what had happened so that the anticipation of their reactions would end. The other part of me wanted to remain numb to avoid seeing what my grief looked like. Would I cry if I allowed myself? I unfortunately chose to let the paranoia stay with me as I put on a happy face, singing cheerful songs in our middle school choir.

I missed school for my grandpa's funeral. The first part of that sentence would normally give me anxiety just thinking about not keeping up my perfect attendance or all of the missed homework that I would have to make up. However, in this time, I was ecstatic to be out of school—away from the constant flow of "I'm-sorry" statements and the ability to be present with my family.

Through my grandpa's wake and funeral service, I found out that I really didn't know him that well. Being the youngest on both sides of my family, I realized that I only had the image of my grandpa as old and having declining health. From the stories my extended family shared, I truly missed him in his prime. I was intrigued as my dad spoke of the childhood he'd had with his now-deceased father; he was now parentless. I then began to feel guilt for not taking the time to make my own lasting memories with my grandpa. I began to have a terrible thought that the funeral would be the most significant memory I'd ever have of this man.

Then I was asked to play piano at his funeral. My mom helped me pick out the hymn as she shared with me, "Grandpa Small loved hearing you play. I don't know if you knew, but he sang in barbershop groups. He also never missed his chance to pull out his harmonica." My mom chuckled as she added, "And he would always be singing or humming along to your piano recitals even if there were no lyrics. I don't think he knew how loud he was sometimes."

Hearing those words from my mom made me feel as though I had a better connection to this mysterious man. No one else in my family shared a passion like mine for music, and I used to wonder why I was so different. If only I had known that my own grandpa walked a similar road as myself, I could have made more lasting memories. That guilt still exists.

Returning to school after the funeral made me feel uneasy. I'd just had my first experience with a loss, saw cousins I had never seen until that point, and heard stories about a man I'd never truly understood. I felt out of place in the school that I had enjoyed spending my days in. My teachers tried their best to bring me back up to speed, but my mind was pulling my body backward from the reality of school. I yearned to be back home and with my mom. Luckily, a couple days after I returned, we had one of the glorious, Wednesday early dismissal school days. I only had to make it past lunchtime, enduring fewer "I'm-sorry-for-your-loss" statements from teachers and friends.

However, a couple things happened that half day of school

that I always think back to as the first gut feelings that I paid attention to. During lunch, I was sitting at a table with two of my friends, Jake and Chris. One was complaining about math or science homework that had been given to us. The other friend was agreeing, continuing to complain more and more, and more, and more, until I shouted.

"Shut up! Are you really going to complain about school when my grandpa just died, and my mom has a life-threatening illness?"

Silence. For a second, I felt as if I'd left my body and I was watching my two friends stare at me in wonder at where this outburst had come from. Chris cut through the awkwardness in a hesitant voice, "How is your mom doing?"

All I could say was that she was fine, but that outburst opened my eyes to the fact that I wasn't. I just experienced the effect of keeping a year's worth of emotions bottled up. I was thankful that day was a half day.

When school was dismissed and I got home, I instantly headed upstairs. I wanted to grab some paint supplies and mindlessly draw, anything that would let me express myself without words. Creativity has always helped me channel my thoughts constructively. As I got up the stairs, I had a second out-of-body feeling where a voice simply said, "Go be with your mom. You never know how much time you have left with her." The voice felt calming, and after my outburst at lunch, I knew I needed to listen to what my mind was saying. So, I decided to lie down in bed where my mom was resting.

My mom simply said, "Please go and have fun. I don't want you to see me like this."

"Mom, I don't care if you are sick. I just enjoy being with you," I said back to her. I noticed tears developing in her eyes. Her furry companion, Pyper, looked up from beside her pillow.

"I know that, but I don't feel well, and I want to get

some rest," she said, crying. I took my cue and slowly went back downstairs to paint. I felt ambivalent over what I'd just experienced.

Although I wasn't able to spend time with her at that moment, I knew I needed to make the attempt to know that I didn't miss any chance to spend more time with her. I didn't want that same guilt I'd had with my grandpa. I wouldn't be able to handle another outburst from harboring all of that guilt. These pivotal moments that I had that day were the start of my gut feelings, feelings that I knew I couldn't ignore, feelings that were beginning to act as my shield.

A week later on a Wednesday, my mom took an unexpected trip to the hospital. I was at home on our computer when I heard my dad leading my mom down the stairs. I remember hearing another person in our house, right inside the door, but my mind was blocking out anything other than me watching my mom slowly make her way to the door. I heard someone say, "Your dad is going to take your mom to Rochester for the night."

I watched our dog, Pyper, uncharacteristically and profusely bark as my mom walked out the door. I wanted to pick Pyper up and let her know everything was all right, but she acted as though she would have bit me if I'd tried. Even after my mom made it outside into the car, Pyper continued her barking fit. As cute as she was, the sound was soul wrenching.

My dad told me that the plan was for me to spend the night at a friend's house. My friend's mom, Jana, who happened to be one of my mom's coworkers, would take me to school the next day. I felt at ease knowing that there was a plan and life would continue as normal going to school the next day. Yet as my dad left to the hospital with my mom, I found it weird that a family friend had come over to help with some household chores. I say "weird" because she took the time to show me exactly what she was doing, teaching me an important life skill—how to do laundry.

As any good plan goes, it changed. My sister, Mallory, had arrived from college, and my other sister and I were going to be headed to the hospital that night. We packed our bags for an overnight trip, and we were in a hurry to leave. I felt flustered. I was starting to feel as if I had not been given the full story—not just for that day but from the start. Her cancer must have spread further than I'd thought. But when you're flustered, what a perfect time for yet another gut feeling!

The voice in my head was telling me, "Bring mom's journal." I didn't think twice, and I grabbed her journal from by the computer. I had remembered seeing this book before when her coworker had given it to her to write in during chemo treatments. I admired the three-dimensional design of trees on the front and back cover, as well as the leather string that tied around the knob in the front. I honestly had never seen her write in this thing, but I wasn't about to ignore another gut feeling.

After an hour-long drive, we made it to the hospital late at night; it was the same hospital that I had visited when I was brave enough to go to that one appointment with my mom. This time, the hospital halls seemed darker than before. Even though it was nighttime on the unit, the atmosphere felt even more uncomfortable than it should have. We walked to my mom's room with our overnight bags in hand, not knowing what we'd be doing with them.

As we entered the room, there were already many people by her side, including my dad. I forget who was all present that night, but I vividly remember taking a seat by the left side of her bed with my dad right across from me. I noticed the machinery my mom was hooked up to, and I remember the noise each made. Most importantly, I noticed the mask on her face, giving her oxygen to breathe.

I grabbed my mom's hand and smiled. She turned her head my way, and through labored breaths, she simply said, "You came." In that moment, I was able to ignore all of the hospital equipment and the uncomfortableness of the room to simply enjoy the time being with my mom. The only conversation I remember hearing after that point was my dad talking about where we kids would be sleeping that night.

I finally looked at the clock to see it was around 1:00 a.m. It was time for the three of us kids to make our way to the connecting hotel. We said our goodbyes to everyone in the room and walked through the halls to our hotel room. As I got in bed, I fell asleep to the surreal moment that we all just experienced.

The next thing I remember was feeling a nudge on my shoulder and the feeling of weight on my bed. I opened my eyes to see the alarm clock read 7:20 a.m. and my mom's friend, Jana, was waking me up. Both of my sisters were already awake on the other bed. Jana looked at each of us.

"Becki fought hard through the night, but she gained her angel wings this morning," Jana told the three of us. I felt each word as she said them and knew they were coming; they were tears.

We all started crying, and Jana wrapped me in a hug. We soon were all embracing each other, crying as much as the rain hitting upon our hotel window. I saw in both of my sisters a natural motherly instinct begin to flourish as they took me under their arms. I understood that they were no longer just my sisters anymore; they had become the closest things I had to a mother figure at that moment.

Additionally, I felt an instinctual switch in myself turn on. The tears stopped, and I knew that the day had to proceed whether I wanted it to or not. There was no more anticipation over the uncertainty. No more anticipatory grief. I had entered full-on grief over our bereavement because the worst had already come, and I was sitting at rock bottom.

My gut feelings attempted to soften the blow of hitting bottom by guiding my actions through the weeks leading up to her death. It still hurt. It hurt to know that exactly two weeks before that Thursday morning, I had answered the phone call at school. My mom could no longer be on the other end.

I remember quickly putting on some clothes, and Jana and some family members took the three of us children to the hospital. Walking through the halls back to her unit, I watched the rain fall outside whenever we passed a window. I oddly had not felt uncomfortable or had the gloomy feeling I had the previous night walking through those halls. Instead, I felt a sense of calmness in myself as I walked into my mom's room. The uncertainty had left.

A priest led us through a final prayer over my mom's body. The calmness continued through that experience. As we were about to leave, though, I frantically remembered that a gut feeling had made me bring something to the hospital. I pulled out my mom's journal from my overnight bag. I untied the leather string from the front cover and opened up the journal.

The journal appeared to be blank. I was confused—until a loose page fell out of it, and I recognized her familiar handwriting:

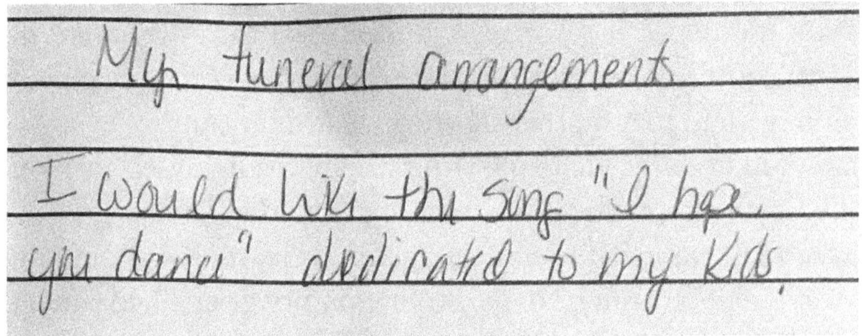

My funeral arrangements

I would like the song "I hope you dance" dedicated to my kids.

Perspective:

THE DAUGHTERS (PART ONE)

Written by Sydney DeMaris & Mallory Nicholson

The hardest part about losing a loved one to a terminal illness was realizing that we weren't told the complete story.

Initial Grief: As Told by Sydney DeMaris

It was my senior year of high school, and I was the typical senior girl—loved hanging out with my friends, "so done" with school, and self-absorbed like no other. Sometimes, I feel angry that I can't remember more details of that entire year of her treatment. I feel as if I was too self-absorbed in high school drama to allow myself to remember some of those moments.

Weirdly, I can remember a different health scare of hers. Some time during my high school career, my mom went in for a typical mammogram. The doctors were concerned about something they saw and wanted to do more tests. We were at the Fourth of July celebration in our town, and we were going to the community lunch at the city park. All she could think about were her tests and what the results might mean. I get my worrying and anxiety from my mom, and you could clearly see it take effect on her that day. The results were all she could focus on because she was worried they would find cancer. Luckily for all of us, everything came back normal, and we went about our lives as usual. That was, until she started to not feel well.

I started noticing that she was always soaking in the tub because she hurt so much. She went about her life and masked the pain as best she could, trying to stay involved in all that she still could with us kids.

My next memory was the day of her diagnosis. I was standing in my room when my dad and mom came upstairs when they were back from the doctors. I could see it in her face that, this time, the results were not good. She hugged me, and all we both could do was bawl our eyes out. My mom and dad didn't tell us much, except that what the doctors had found was, in fact, cancer.

I went about my life, I guess. I tried to forget the reality that she had this disease. As she became more and more sick and was spending more and more time at home on the couch or in bed, I avoided the house like the plague. I was literally afraid to be around her. I didn't want to have to see her in pain, and I didn't know what to say or do to help. Being with her, being away from her—they both made me afraid.

In her last month, she was in bed most of the day. She was too exhausted to do anything. Yet as I was lying in bed one day, she came into my room and laid down next to me. She didn't say much, just laid there. I was eating candy at the time, and strangely, I even remember what kind of candy—Now and Laters. Together, we just laid there, eating my Now and Laters in silence. I don't know why that moment sticks out in my head, but it does. Maybe I remember that moment because for once, I didn't feel scared; I was just enjoying being with her.

Initial Grief: As Told by Mallory Nicholson

It was Christmas break, and I was a freshman in college. I was waiting at home for my parents to come back with my mom's test results. I never felt we got the whole story on her health because we were kids, but nonetheless, I was impatiently waiting to go back to college that same day once we found out the news.

They came back home and confirmed it was cancer. I don't think she knew the full details at that time, but I just remember feeling numb. I didn't understand what was going on. I was also sad because I didn't know what I would rather have had: having to be at home like the rest of my family and watch her go through this; or having to be far away from home and figure out these emotions by myself.

College is a lonely place, especially your freshman year in a dorm. After finding out she had cancer, I had to be rushed back into college life. I didn't have my car with me, and my boyfriend, Matt, was miles away at another college. Matt's mother, Mary, had to be the one to drive me home that day, and I remember her saying how hard of an experience that was for her.

"This is someone who found out her mother has cancer and here I am leaving her at a college dorm, alone," she told me years later. Apparently, she cried the whole way home. I don't know if I cried when I got to my dorm because I wasn't sure if the news would be too awkward for my roommate. I doubt I told her. I just kept it in and was alone in my initial grief.

When I was home for the summer or during breaks, I

started to see a little of her decline. There were times that I had to be the one to take her to her appointments. Often, we were at the Mayo Clinic in Rochester, Minnesota, the whole day, going through appointment after appointment. She was sometimes almost giddy and excited, showing me off and introducing me to her PA. "This is my daughter," and, "Have you met my daughter? This is the Mallory I've been talking about!"

Her excitement and entire demeanor changed after radiation, though. She was wiped out, which meant I had to drive her home. I didn't think anything at the time, but I realize now how sad it was. I was seeing the decline. Going to the hospital, she was a strong person; but leaving treatment, that strength was gone.

Then, one day, we were shopping and trying on shoes. This was just before she died. She leaned over to me and started saying, "Don't tell Sydney and Sawyer, but …." She was alluding to the fact that she was having more pain in her back. I remember thinking, Wait, what does that mean? She told me that the doctors thought the cancer had moved to her bones. She was letting me in on things she wasn't telling my siblings because I was little bit older. I think she needed someone to say something to, but at the same time, I was only nineteen. She didn't want to let me in on everything, leaving her passing away to still be a big surprise. Her disclosure in the shoe store left me thinking, This is reality. This is actually happening.

Anticipatory Grief: As Told by Sydney DeMaris

The day before she died, I came home from school to find another one of my mom's friends helping around the house and folding laundry. Soon, more people started to come over.

One of her friends told me that she wasn't feeling well, and they were going to try and get her to the hospital. They had trouble getting her down the stairs, though, because she was having trouble breathing. Before she left, through labored breathing, she said, "Bye, I love you." I was in shock. I couldn't comprehend what was going on.

I had to go to a night class, but all I could do was pace the driveway before I left, thinking, Can I make it through this class without crying? Should I go, or should I be staying home in case something happens?

I went to class and I made it through—barely. I didn't talk much to anyone and headed straight out the door to my car when class ended. My good friend stopped me and asked if I knew that my mom had gone to the hospital. The news must have already spread to her mom. A simple, "Yes," was all I could say. My friend then informed me, though, that she'd heard my grandma and grandpa had headed to the hospital as well. Time just stood still from that moment on. Maybe that was the point when I realized that this was really serious, something was going to happen.

I returned home to more of my mom's friends. They informed me that they were waiting for Mallory to come back from college, and they would take us to see our mom.

Throughout the whole car ride, I just kept playing scenarios over in my head. My emotions were all over the place. I was worried, sad, anxious, and angry—at myself and others. Why did I avoid her so much? Why didn't I spend more time with her? I was angry at my mom and dad because they downplayed her cancer. They knew how advanced the cancer was, and not once did they ever tell me. I understand now why they did it, but in the days preceding and following her death, I was angry. I was also mad at God. I thought, Why her? Why should I believe in someone that would put anyone through this—especially someone who is so great to me?

Finally, we got to Rochester and were greeted at the hospital by more of our family. I hated seeing my mom that way. To this day, that's not how I want to remember her—hooked up to machines to help her breath and lying there in so much pain as if she was holding on just for us. I didn't want to be there, but I didn't want to *not* be there. While I sat there, I kept staring at her, from her eyes and then to the air forcing itself into her and making her whole body move up and down.

Mom was lying there, with sad eyes and staring at all of us. My young, innocent brother was talking to her as if nothing was wrong, "Guess what? I get to go to the bookstore to get a book tomorrow."

I was so upset with him at the time. Why would you be talking about books at a time like this? I soon realized that this was his way of dealing. We all had to find ways to deal.

Experiencing the Death: As Told by Mallory Nicholson

Two weeks before my mom died, I was studying for midterms, and I received the call from her that my grandpa had passed away. In the midst of the sadness, I remember being so stressed about college and initially thinking, What am I going to do? I have things to do and places to be.

Then, when my dad called me a couple weeks later on that Wednesday and said that my mom wasn't doing well, I again thought, But I have a test tomorrow and another on Friday. What am I supposed to do? I was once again studying but didn't know how serious the situation was and if I could do anything.

My dad called a second time. "Cassondra is going to pick you up and take you halfway. Laurie and Lori will then meet you and take you home so you can ride with Sydney and Sawyer to Rochester." A whirlwind of directions.

I got off the phone and had a lot to process. This haunted me for a while because the only thing that I could think was, "Well, I can't go! I have a test to take. How am I going to make this all work? Now, I have to email the professor and …" I was thinking about myself, and that became hard for me after she passed away because I was mad at myself for thinking more about school in that moment.

When we got to the hospital, I remember holding her hand through the bed railings. My arm was hurting so much, but it's one of those things—you just don't let go. She really wanted us to leave and for my dad to take us to a hotel. I was trying to make light of the situation and started rubbing her hair. I noticed her heart rate was going down when I did that. I thought, Oh, it's helping! I don't even think it ever registered what was going on. I didn't think anything was going to happen. I was just relieved when we finally went to bed.

Next thing I remember was waking up and looking at the clock, which read 7:00 a.m. Sydney was also awake and said that she woke up suddenly—not because of any noise or alarm or person. Like me, she just felt something. Then we received a knock at the door. Our uncle and mom's friend came in to give us the devastating news. I went to the bathroom and cried, instantly calling Matt and waking him up on that dreary morning. Despite being in the midst of his own midterms, he said he was going to drive home to see me after he took an exam that morning.

It was rainy and gross that day, and not everything had hit me yet. I wasn't numb to emotions because I had been able to cry. I just wanted to get back home as soon as we could, but I ended up becoming so annoyed because our mom's friend,

Becky, took us kids to Barnes & Noble. Sawyer *had* to go and get a book before we went home.

Sydney and I became angry. "Why would you do this!" On top of that, as we were leaving the bookstore, someone had opened up the door for us as we were leaving and had said, "Have a nice day!" I looked at this stranger with the most disgusted and confused face, thinking, Have a nice day? My mom just died. You're an idiot! Still to this day, I think about those things we say to strangers and how something that may seem like a normal greeting or phrase could cause so much negative emotions. You never know what someone has been going through that day.

Luckily, when I had to return to college immediately after her funeral, my professor was a little more sensitive to my traumatic experience and let me have more time to take the test. I was relieved to know that at least I didn't need to be so stressed about my schoolwork. I didn't need to be haunted by the fact that college was what I was worrying about throughout her death. I was instead haunted for weeks by nightmares of the image we saw of her after she had passed. I couldn't shake that image from my head for a while, but it had helped when I heard that these types of dreams are the brain's way of registering that the person has actually passed. The meaning of the dream was to tell me that she was no longer present in that shell of an image; she had been set free.

3 The Butterfly Effect

The hardest part about finding meaning in grief is recognizing the signs that were right in front of you.

"Meaning makes a great many things endurable—perhaps everything."[1] This quote from the late psychiatrist and psychoanalyst Carl Jung resonates well with my own life. Like my mom, I've always liked to keep things organized and straight—including my thoughts (and, hopefully, this book). The hardest part about finding meaning in grief and keeping those thoughts straight, however, is knowing where to begin.

I used to hate the phrase "everything happens for a reason." That phrase gets thrown around as a go-to sentence when trying to comfort another person who is experiencing a difficult situation. My mom used that phrase with me when I experienced my first breakup. I have used it with friends for various trivial reasons, not realizing how disingenuous I was being. After having to hear the phrase said to you, though, you start to understand why people may roll their eyes when you unwittingly profess this belief that there is a bigger picture in mind.

"Everything happens for a reason" is a phrase that's meant to give a positive outlook that there is a meaning behind all of the suffering, a method to the madness. Someday you will learn why you had to go through this or how this specific event will lead you to a better path. In some situations, I like using the phrase because it implies a faith-filled message that life will, in fact, get better. In the case of losing a loved one, though, I was having a hard time finding the meaning behind why my family needed to experience an event such as my mom's death. I wanted that phrase forever banned from my vernacular.

However, that phrase is not the worst that can be said when it comes to losing a loved one. If you have already experienced a loss, or when you do, you will begin to just hate any phrase that you hear too often. It's true that some people may say the most insensitive things while you are vulnerable due to their lack of experience with what you are going through, but even the simplest of sentences can become annoying. As I experienced with my grandpa, I didn't like hearing, "I'm sorry for your loss"—one of the most commonly used phrases with a death. I didn't like this phrase because to me, it meant that other people were becoming upset over the fact that I was upset. I didn't want to be the reason why more people were in a depressed mood. Should I fake being happier to make it all better, then?

No matter what phrases you hear and which ones you get sick of, the fact of the matter is that the grief journey has begun. The day my mom died, I felt all of the anticipation of the worst-case scenario dissolve as we realized we had finally arrived at that scenario, the climax in our story. I now know that the calm I experienced that early morning of her death was because I was released from the hold of anticipatory grief. It was a brief sense of calm, but also a chance to dissociate from the long-term grief that was setting in. The moment I returned from my calm, I began my search for any meaning behind the grief my family was subjected to. Luckily, I had my mom's journal to begin that process.

Scrolling through her journal once again after leaving my mom's hospital room, I realized that she'd barely touched it. The journal was intended for her to write her journey through treatment. Instead, she inserted a single, loose piece of paper in it that acted as her funeral planner, letting us know how we could best honor her wishes. In typical Becki fashion, she had continued writing further on that page how she wanted to be different than anyone else by requesting a specific meal for the after-funeral lunch—hot beef sandwiches and corn—as opposed to the traditional lackluster meal everyone else gets. More importantly, though, her funeral planning gave us a glimpse into what she wanted to say the most before she passed—how her children could remember her.

Slipping the journal back into my overnight bag, we proceeded to go have brunch with all of our family who were present at the hospital. My mind was still not registering all that had just happened within the previous hours. I just remember staring outside the window whenever I could and admiring the overcast sky and the light rainfall. The cool sensation of an April shower, the smell, and the sense of cleansing that came with the rain made me feel at ease—even just for a little bit.

She enjoyed storms. A rainy day was what relaxed her, and despite the terrible consequences of natural disasters, she had admitted that thunderstorms—especially tornadoes—were fascinating. She had taken me outside during a storm, and we had both been captivated by the swirling clouds above our heads, wind blowing against our skin. "Isn't this beautiful?" she had asked. I couldn't help but smile at the fitting atmosphere the world brought on the day my mother entered eternal peace.

The day she died is another memory still vivid to me, because with every action I took, I knew I would be looking back to that very moment later on. I may have been surrounded by family and friends, but I was very much in my own mind, focused on processing what was next.

"Well, it looks like you inherited a phone today," my dad said, leaning toward me at brunch. He handed me my mom's phone, and I wasn't sure what to think. I had begged my mom for that past year to let me buy my own phone in order to work around the no-phone-until-you-are-sixteen law in our household. If this phone was the explanation for "everything happening for a reason," then I wanted to return this to its sender.

A family friend, Becky, drove me and my siblings home that morning. Despite all of the action going on around me with my dad beginning the early planning of a funeral, family friends coming in and out of the house, and my sisters doing whatever they were doing, I went straight for the computer. In this time where all the emotions were unfamiliar, I went toward something that I was familiar with—music. My mom's journal page gave me the inspiration and first song to compile a CD of "Becki's Songs" that could be given out to family and friends as a remembrance. I was on a mission to find my meaning through music.

Within a couple of hours of working on the CD, however, Jana brought her son, Caden, over to be with me. Caden was one of my best friends at the time, and he came bearing a gift—a cappuccino from my favorite gas station. It was the same beverage that my mother had gotten me hooked on. In that moment, I had found some immediate comfort.

The simple presence of being with a friend allowed me to be myself and feel like a kid again.

As the day turned to night, more and more friends started to appear at my door. I knew that my school had announced my mom's death to the students and faculty that day, but I felt as if there was some distress call shining in the night sky for my classmates to be there for me that night. Part of me wished to keep working on my mom's CD and be among the rest of my family as they discussed funeral plans, but a bigger part of me wanted to get away and feel like a fourteen-year-old.

Soon, what began as friends coming to simply visit me, turned into a night of videotaping all of us lip-synching to songs and making ridiculous music videos in the upstairs of my house. I still watch these videos today because if I didn't already know, I wouldn't have guessed that these videos were filmed on the day my mother died. I felt as if I was watching myself just be a normal teenager despite the disarray that was going on a floor below me with the rest of my family processing their emotions. But, deep down, I knew that that was what my mother wanted for me on that day—to simply have fun and be in the presence of friends. The time for processing would soon come in the following days.

That next morning, my family met with the funeral director. My instinctual switch turned on again, and I felt myself emotionally in the body of an adult as we were discussing her wake and funeral service. I wasn't bothered by missing school, I didn't bother to cry as we discussed the coming days, and I wasn't bothered as I watched other family members tear up. I was on a mission to make my voice heard, give my mom the tribute she deserved, and to bring her journal wishes to light.

"I am so proud of the kids for being so active in all of

this," I overheard Laura, my aunt, say to my other aunt, Terri, as we sat in the basement of the funeral home.

I was able to complete the *Becki's Songs* CD, and we had these songs playing in the background of the wake service. As people made their way through the long line of the wake, they were able to listen to Becki's tribute during their wait, commenting how "special" it was to hear. My memory of the wake service ended with a special moment between my dad and me as we cried to the song "I Swear"[2]—the song that my mom had sung to me when I was younger.

From her wishes, "I Hope You Dance"[3] was included as a tribute to the three of us kids and was played at the end of the funeral service. Every time the song played, I felt as if she was singing right to me. I admit, though, that I wasn't quite sure what she meant with those words or why she chose that song in particular. She wasn't even a fan of country music. I just understood that each time I heard it, there was a special meaning she was trying to convey to her children. One day I wanted to find that meaning.

The last tribute I had requested was to play piano once again to the mother who'd supported my musical dreams. As I did exactly two weeks before at my grandfather's funeral, I played the same hymn while family and friends sat and reminisced on the unique personality that was Becki. I remember thinking, Thank God this piano is facing the wall, and I don't have to look at anyone in this congregation. Just close your eyes and play.

As the sound of the piano echoed through the church, I realized that I had at least found meaning behind why my mom wanted to pick out the hymn for my grandpa's funeral; she knew I would need it again. I also became aware in that moment that the music was better than any words I could muster up. I knew that I could channel any emotion into what I was playing and have those thoughts be conveyed to everyone present; a sense of calm yet again.

* * *

As the events of her death started to settle down and I was hearing fewer and fewer "I'm-sorry-for-your-loss" statements every day, I felt an awkward transition back into the real world. The back-to-back deaths put me in an unnatural routine, making the change of going to school so abrupt. I wasn't ready to stop thinking about my mother. Why had people stopped talking about her all of a sudden? Why was it a taboo subject, now? I mean, wasn't everyone just talking about her, reminiscing about their experiences with her, and offering support for me and my family? This mum effect, as psychologists have put it, created a silence that hurt worse than words.[4]

As much as I thought I hated hearing people use their various phrases to comfort me, I hated the silence even more. There was at least a sense of "I'm-thinking-of-you-and-your-family" when she was brought up. When others skirted around the subject or avoided using her name, it felt like I'd never had a mom. Even the "yo-mama" jokes that were so popular in the 2000s were stopped midsentence around me. Are we just going to pretend that she didn't exist, guys?

She did more than exist, though; she was the reason I existed, and she was more than present all the time with her family and friends. She would be the first person to console you when you were feeling upset or sick. I often wondered how my mom could exert so much energy for other people without going crazy herself, but yet, she was always there.

The statement that best explained her empathy and presence came one day when I was at my aunt Laura's house. My dad and my aunt reminisced about how my mom used to view dragonflies as her deceased brother, Mike, visiting her from beyond the grave. My mom was then quoted saying, "If I die, I will come back as a butterfly and be with my family and friends—always and forever." I heard these words and my eyes widened, ears perked up, and the paranormal geek in me was ecstatic to hear that there may be some way that my mom could be with me.

Ever since the day she died, I was looking for any sign I could that she was with me, or at least pulling one of her usual pranks. I kept hearing stories from family members and her friends of little weird occurrences that had happened shortly after her death. I had heard too many stories about "supernatural" activity such as when one of the few picture frames of her and her siblings fell off the wall at my grandmother's house; or the story that my dad told of a family of geese blocking the interstate on the morning she died, causing the caravan of vehicles to stop until they passed; and lastly, the even crazier story of a mysterious card that my mom had written in the hospital suddenly appearing on her friend, Lori's, desk one day but gone the next time Lori went to grab it.

Everyone was looking for the butterflies and viewed any sighting of one as her presence. They were trying to find meaning in their grief through these simple little creatures. "A butterfly flew by my car window today," or, "There were two butterflies on a flower outside my work and I thought of your mom," were just a couple of common statements I would hear. Butterfly flower holders were even placed at her gravestone at all times. They were everywhere.

I was a little upset at not having had one of these experiences because I had always loved the idea of the supernatural, but then again, how were these butterflies special in any way? Where was the meaning in it? These "sightings" were no different than viewing the sun or the moon as examples of why God was with us each and every day. They were too common. Plus, my mom was more grandeur than that. You would have known if she was with you.

After trying to talk to my mom at night and asking for a special sign just for me, I still wasn't receiving any message. I decided to give up on that hope and realized that the whole "butterfly effect" was just a simple way of remembering her—nothing out of the ordinary. I didn't really need a sign, did I? I at least still saw her in my dreams, despite how weird and cryptic those dreams were. My mind was clearly still keeping her in my memory and I would never forget the impact she made on me.

There, I learned the secret of getting over grief. I wondered, Can I move on, now?

However, when a year rolled around on her anniversary, I woke up to a thunderstorm. I opened my window, stared outside, and smiled to myself, feeling once again the cleansing nature of the sound, smell, and sights of nature's doing. I started to think, Maybe this was the sign she left for me. It rained on the day she died.

Thunderstorms were something we both shared a love for. So, why couldn't I enjoy these rainy moments that clearly show that she is remembered? Oddly enough, just about every year so far after her death, April 10 brought a thunderstorm at some point in the day. On those first couple of anniversaries, I started to think, Thank you, Mom, for giving me a way of celebrating your anniversary as opposed to dreading the date each year.

The thunderstorms taught me to calm my nerves and relieve the symptoms of my anxiety. They brought me the calm feeling that helped me feel as if I was acknowledging my grief and continuing to find meaning through it. I certainly was understanding the reason why my mom enjoyed them, which made me feel closer to her than I had since she died. I think I'm getting a handle of all of this, I thought, finally. At least, I was until history wanted to repeat itself.

* * *

"Did you hear about Caden's mom?" a friend asked me in school.

"No," I responded, puzzled. "Is Jana all right?"

"Her cancer is back, I guess. Everyone's been talking about it. Remember when she was bald back in elementary school because of all of the treatment? Ugh ... I hope that doesn't happen to her again. Scary, isn't it?"

"Yeah. You're telling me," I responded, already worried about what this information meant to me. My friend was right, though. The whole school had been talking about Jana's brain tumor because she was a beloved paraprofessional who'd worked alongside my mom in the elementary school. When my class—which included her son, Caden—had been in third grade, she was undergoing treatment to get rid of her brain tumor. Through radiation, they were able to shrink it down to a size that they could safely remove.

Less than ten years later, my class was hearing the same news about her tumor. I was optimistic, though. If she could fight the cancer off once, she could do it again! Caden and his younger sister, Jadee, had both inherited Jana's positive attitude. They were there for me with my mother's treatment and death, remaining positive for me the whole time. I wanted to do the same for them.

As Jana started receiving treatment again, my family and the friends of Jana were kept in the loop about her progress. We wanted to know how and when we could help because Jana always did the same when it came to others. Luckily, I had a phone now that could allow me to keep in touch with her. However, in the midst of her treatment, she was the one who decided to reach out to me, texting me a simple picture. I opened my phone to these words:

> "Receiving treatment today. Found this outside my ten-story room window. Your mom is with me."

I couldn't believe what I was seeing. I had been wrong about the butterflies. It was more than just seeing a butterfly on any spring day. It was about these special butterflies with a hidden and calming meaning. The butterfly effect was real, and I now understood that the butterflies were meant to help me through any grief I would experience in the future. I'll happily take the support wherever I can get it.

Perspective:

THE SISTER

Written by LeAnne Wagner

The hardest part about losing a sister is simply living my life without her and her support.

Becki and I had the typical sisterly relationship. She was always kicking me off couches, pulling my hair, or pinching me with her toes. As teens, we fought as most sisters would, as we were the only ones left in the house. She was more interested in boys and girl stuff, while I was always playing sports, swimming, or something like that. She was part of what I considered the cool crowd in high school—popular, had a boyfriend, a job, and everyone liked her. I was always shy and didn't consider myself a "partier." I looked up to her, though, because she never gave me a hard time for not being like her, despite others wondering if we were truly sisters, considering we were interested in different things.

She had her way of making people smile by doing mischievous things. She mooned people, showed her food while she was chewing, farted—anything that would catch you off guard and elicit a smile. I can't count the number of times she walked into a room with her pajamas on (a red 5k race shirt), and she quickly lifted up her shirt in front of me before going about her business. She had a great combination of my dad's sense of humor and my mom's moxie. But she also knew how to be sweet and caring through acts such as surprising me with balloons and a cookie cake when I landed my first teaching job.

One of my best memories of our relationship was when she came to watch me play in a regional final volleyball match before she went off to college. This was extremely important to me because our team wanted to get to the state tournament. She came and sat with our mom and dad and cheered louder than anyone. Despite losing a suspenseful match, Becki said through a hoarse voice, "That match was so exciting!" It felt like she was with me every step of the way, proud of my performance and effort. Her being there meant the world to me, and it felt like we had made a large step toward an "adult" sibling relationship. This relationship, to me, was better than sisters—we were friends.

Therefore, I wanted to make sure that I didn't miss out on any time with Becki and her family. I did the same thing I did with Mike, my older brother, before he died—I visited as often as I could because I didn't want to look back and say, "I wish …" I was anticipating the worst. So, I made the decision to try and get back home every other weekend as much as I could with work and other commitments because Becki took priority! I looked forward to seeing everyone and spending time with my family because I wanted to have those memories regardless of what happened.

Going back home to Illinois, however, was harder each time—especially as she was declining and in such pain. I often spent the ride back, crying off and on. Dawn, one of my colleagues and friends, usually called me to see if I was on my way back. "Maybe you shouldn't go," she once said.

"You hurt too much, and you're a mess when you get back." I know she was trying to protect me from going through the pain, but there was no way that I wasn't going to visit. Nothing I went through was any worse than what Becki endured—fighting for her life—and what her family endured seeing her go through that on a daily basis.

I also tried calling Becki regularly. As she declined, though, she didn't feel like talking, or she was always resting. This is when I talked to her husband, Bruce. I appreciated those discussions as a chance for me to talk, as well as a chance for him to talk. I always have considered Bruce my brother, knowing him longer than the time I had with my own brother, Mike. So, I needed to be there for Bruce.

He called me the night Becki was taken to Rochester, Minnesota. He told me what had happened, but I could tell that he wasn't sure if this was "it" or not. When I got off the phone, I went to work on my lesson plans, writing a week's worth of sub notes because I was planning on leaving in the morning to head to either Iowa or Minnesota. I didn't know how long I would be gone. I lost it on the phone with a colleague as I let her know where she could find everything for school when I left. Then Bruce called again. I don't remember the conversation, but I'm sure in his heart he knew that this would be it, but he didn't want to make the decision whether I should hurry or not.

I waffled back and forth on whether I should leave as soon as I hung up or wait until morning. I chose to wait—telling myself and Bruce that I didn't want to drive that late, being tired and upset, especially since I was by myself. When I hung up, it only took me a few minutes to get sick; not something that happens to me very often. I think everything together upset my stomach so much, so I threw up. I was crying and exhausted and I tried to sleep—getting minimal. I woke up relatively early so that I could call work and let them know what was happening, I packed my bags for what I thought might be a funeral, and I was ready to leave when my mom finally called: Becki had died.

I felt what I considered "sad relief." It wasn't that I was relieved that she'd died. It's just that when you are living life with something like that hanging over you, it's hard not to feel relieved when it's gone. I didn't feel guilt for that feeling. I'm sure it's pretty normal and doesn't have anything to do with whether or not I loved Becki. I just took some time to rest before I started driving. I laid on the couch and turned on the TV while contemplating what my life was going to be like without her. Somehow having the TV on at all times makes me feel not as alone—hearing its voices. It was my time to come to grips with this change and what was the beginning of a long grieving process.

My biggest concern as I arrived home, and eventually to Becki's house, was whether or not Becki knew that I loved her. I remember breaking down and crying with Bruce and asking him if he told her I loved her. I'm sure I had asked him to tell her for me. I had somewhat of a panic attack that I didn't say goodbye to her or get to tell her that I loved her—that I would miss her. I didn't want her to feel that I'd abandoned her at the end. Hopefully there were other things that I did that showed her how much she meant to me, but this ambiguity and uncertainty ate away at me.

After the wake service, I remember going out to my car and getting in it to drive. That's when it hit me—another devastating feeling of pain. I felt my heart was broken at that moment. It was an overwhelming feeling that gives me shivers today to think about. I had never felt a true heartbreaking feeling until that moment. I was almost frozen in time and couldn't help but feel that the world as I knew it had changed forever. It's a lonely feeling, and it definitely overwhelmed me for some time, creeping up another time at Sydney's graduation party as we were trying to locate the quilt my mom had made for her. Becki would have been able to tell us exactly where it was.

I had to kick the habit of picking up my cell phone and calling her. It was difficult to change a habit of calling your best friend and sister to share news, as she was sometimes my first and only call. I also had to kick another habit. I couldn't sleep in my bed for quite a while after Becki died. I don't know why. I slept on my couch for about six months after, eventually forcing myself to go to bed in my bedroom. This was probably something very similar to why I turn on the TV. Somehow sleeping on my couch was more comforting than my bed because maybe sleeping on the couch was more *hopeful* than going to bed.

Overall, right after her death I guess you could say that I was depressed. I was functioning, going to work, and so on, but not very well. One of my bosses pulled me into her office one day after she observed me in my classroom. She was concerned because I was "flat," and she felt like I wasn't enjoying teaching anymore. "Do you have anything in your life that brings you joy?" she asked.

I started to cry a bit and said, "No." This was a watershed moment for me. Here I was being told that I wasn't doing a very good job teaching. My boss knew what I had been through, and she knew that I needed help, telling me to seek out the counsel of a therapist to try and find my way back to being myself. I needed to find the meaning in all of this grief.

I did see a therapist for a couple of months after that. It's funny, though, I didn't think that we talked about anything earth-shattering, but after we were finished with the sessions, I felt better. I felt like I could find joy in something again. I started to think about what would bring that joy to me. This is when I started making changes.

I went back to school for a second master's degree—this

time with a focus on educational technology. Upon finishing the degree, I actively looked for jobs in that field and was offered the job at Catalyst Charter in Chicago. I moved to Chicago, got a dream job, and started over. It's not that I didn't like living in the Quad Cities area, but I felt that I needed to pursue a change in my career so that I could be excited and passionate about the work I did daily again.

I was also coming to a bigger conclusion that had been happening for a while. I think I had always had a suspicion that I was gay. I dismissed the thought in high school and college and was still looking for that special someone when I moved to the Quad Cities area. However, I started to realize in my late twenties and early thirties that the only connections that I seemed to make were with women. So, I started to question again, whether or not I was gay.

I can remember the conversation I had with myself. I was driving and finally said it out loud: "I'm gay." This was soon followed by, "Okay, well, no one needs to know." I had admitted it to myself, which is a huge step, but I wasn't ready to share it with anyone. However, after Becki's sickness and death, I realized that I could no longer live my life without being myself. I had been given a fresh start moving to Chicago, and I had been able to live "out" among my new colleagues. I was slowly feeling more comfortable to begin telling my friends and family.

"Oh, I knew that! Becki and I used to talk about it all the time. Becki used to wonder if *you* knew you were gay," my sister, Laura, said. Along with my mom, I was hearing more of these statements. It seemed that I was the last to know. I must say that I felt better knowing that Becki knew that I was gay. It comforts me to know that because she didn't treat me any differently—she loved me for who I am, and if she had lived, she would've been the first one I would have told. She would have been in my corner.

Then, I began to ponder. Becki and I had talked about love and dating once—not something we talked about a lot. She told me, "You know, you are going to meet that special someone, and it will be instant. You are going to be one of those people who doesn't need to date a lot of people. When you meet that person, they will be the one." I think about that now. She didn't say meet the "man" of my dreams. She was giving me the faith that someday I would be able to share my life with someone. She was saying that, whatever I can do to be happy, I should do it.

And do it I shall. Upon changing careers and locations, I also began my weight-loss journey. Becki and I had both gone through Weight Watchers[1] together, and both had success at times. She was an invaluable resource for me to keep me going, but my weight got substantially worse than hers ever had. However, within two years of sticking to a new program, I was able to lose 150 pounds. I feel great! There's more I would like to work on, but it helps to know that whenever I am looking for Becki's support, I am able to put on her red 5k race shirt. I feel like she is with me every step of the way.

There is not a day that goes by that I don't think of Becki. It might be something that reminds me of her or something that happens and I think, Becki would've loved that, or, I wish I could tell Becki about this. That will never go away. You learn to deal with this feeling, and I've learned that it even brings a smile to my face most times. It's part of what makes me, me. Some of the painful memories begin to fade, so I guess age is not a bad thing when it comes to losing some of those memories.

As time has passed, I've found some meaning in my grief. Although it took a little longer than with my brother, Mike, I started seeing Becki in my dreams. I always felt that their appearance in my dreams was a good sign that my grief was starting to ease up a bit. I still have the regret of not visiting sooner that last day and telling Becki I loved her, but I have to practice self-compassion, knowing that I made the decision that I needed for myself at that time. Thus, making visits home whenever I can comforts me and helps me cope when I'm missing her.

I even have both dragonfly and gerbera daisy tattoos in honor of Mike and Becki to help me remember all of those positive memories. Although, Becki has her own way of making sure I remember her. In my first day at my new job, I was sitting in my new office—taking in the view around me. I had my window open, and a butterfly flew into my office. It was her. I know it. She was letting me know that she was still supporting me, cheering me on through a hoarse voice.

The grief of losing two siblings has shaped my life as much as anything else. I just have to make sure that I grow from it and not let it tear me down by bottling up all of my grief. I found that I needed to have faith in good things in order to survive, and I think that was part of the reason why I didn't react in anger with Becki's illness and death.

I still have lots of questions about what comes after this life, and that always causes some angst for me, but I want to believe that we will all be together again. That's what I try to hold on to during times of grief because grief is simply like everything else—weight loss and coming out—it's all a process that each person handles differently.

4 High School (The) Musical

The hardest part about keeping grief bottled up is picking yourself back up in the inevitable aftermath of the explosion.

Developing coping strategies can be a process. When you experience a loss of any kind, you will be faced with a question: How am I going to handle this? There are temporary fixes, such as avoiding that person's room and possessions, avoiding your own room, or taking a nap when the grief gets too intense. These quick fixes will only be effective up until a certain point. Finding your long-term coping strategies will help you process through your grief more effectively.

I came across a unique passage in a book that stated that even the best coping strategies can eventually become defective if you allow that strategy to be maintained even after it has done its job.[1] For example, taking a hot bath to soothe anxiety is an acceptable coping strategy, but can become maladaptive if the length and frequency of taking a hot bath interferes with daily work or schedules. Taking a nap to relieve your mind, avoiding your loved one's possessions, or avoiding sleeping in your own bed allows you to keep your emotions stable for a time, but eventually you will need to address the emotions to regain your sense of security.

The author of this book passage, Ruth Bright, added, "If this coping mechanism becomes permanent and the stress is never dealt with, adverse effects that may be resistant to change usually follow."[2]

I had found my temporary fixes between the butterflies and thunderstorms. I could argue that these eventually became adaptable and lasting coping strategies, but in the first few years, they were being used as temporary solutions and excuses to not express my emotions to others. I was yearning for any type of connection that could link me back to being with her. This was my grief. I was simply trying to go back to the days where I could always go to my mom for any type of advice.

Why did I prefer my mom's advice? Simply, I had always been a "mama's boy" in all ways. Through birth all the way to middle school, my mother and I had been inseparable. Granted, I still had "father-and-son time" with my dad whenever we went fishing or if I helped him at his auto shop, but I had always chosen to run to my mom when I needed someone to talk to. I had shared anything personal with her and, sometimes to my downfall, even my elementary and middle school crushes. I clearly remember a time when a couple of my "crushes" had admitted to me that my mom had shared my interest of them to their mothers. She truly had been the queen of embarrassment.

Silly enough, I've also heard that, after having my two sisters, she had been desperately hoping to have a boy. Apparently, she'd tried all the "special tips and tricks" to hopefully have her third and final child be a boy. She even kept my gender a secret among my dad and my aunt LeAnne once she knew. Needless to say, the bond we'd had had been strong because I had been able to see the unconditional love she'd had for not only me, but her whole family. She had been my obvious choice in who to trust with my prepubescent struggles.

Soon after her death, stepping in to high school presented an abrupt change for me. High school in general is a time for people to find their interests, grow in their independence, figure out general directions for where they want to go in life, and—to be honest—let themselves fall down many times. In order to fall down, however, you have to be willing to put yourself out there. I was learning that the difference between my middle school years and these four years of high school were that I wouldn't have my confidante to run to whenever I did fall down. I needed to find another way to make it through, hopefully not just a quick fix.

By the time I started high school, both of my sisters were already in college, leaving the once full house to dwindle down to my dad and myself. On the bright side, I got to move into a bigger room and change my old one into a music room. On the other side, I remember thinking, Does this mean I only have Dad I can talk to?

I knew the answer to that question was that there were other friends and family willing to listen, but I took the option of deciding to avoid emotional processing at all. I wasn't ready to take what I had with my mom and force that type of relationship onto my dad. I had once heard the idea that grief wouldn't be able to change the type of relationship you have with someone, but it would surely intensify the relationship that you had with that person prior to the death you experienced together. Therefore, if my dad and I didn't open up to each other before, how could I expect that to change after her death?

Looking back, I know my dad would have embraced that type of relationship, but I felt uncomfortable. I wasn't ready to have what I had with my mom with him, and I didn't need to as long as I had thunderstorms and butterflies to stay connected with my mom. Unfortunately, culture also made me believe there was something unnatural about discussing emotions with a paternal figure, even if my dad and I were often sensitive people. I instead found myself snapping at him easily when he tried to make his way into my world of grief.

Thus, I was still searching for connections to my mom. My logical choice was to distract myself with the activity that she'd always supported, which was music. When I asked to start piano lessons at age six, my mom had been hesitant because my sisters, or at least one, had decided to quit gymnastics. My mom had worried that I would waste time and money on something I would eventually quit. Possibly through giving her the puppy dog eyes or because she had been able to tell music was what I needed, she'd finally let me take lessons.

As the years went by, she'd become my biggest supporter with music because she'd seen how much I enjoyed playing and practicing. She'd enjoyed taking me to lessons to hear my progress and essentially had become my at-home teacher due to knowing what my piano teacher had wanted me to work on. She'd even located a beautiful and blond used piano to put in our home shortly after I'd started taking piano lessons. When I joined band as a percussionist, she'd helped me find a drum to practice with at home. When I'd decided to try out for state choirs in middle school, she had made sure I had been signed up for the camps to help. She'd wanted to feed my new passion.

I still recall a conversation I had with one of my classmates at a soccer game, which showed how my mom had chosen to *publicly* support my endeavors:

"Hey, Sawyer, my mom and I ran into your mom at the grocery store. She was hilarious. She was all like, 'My goodness, I can't believe Sawyer made the honor choir. What a nerd!'" my friend Sam had said while laughing.

I'd smiled and said, "Classic Becki."

I will always associate my passion for music with my mother because, besides the jokes or ways she had used music to embarrass me, I knew how emotionally invested she had been in helping me use my talents. The first time I publicly sang at one of my piano recitals, I hid the fact that I would be singing as well. My piano teacher and I even perfectly timed it so that I would practice that song during lessons when my mom stepped outside to get stuff from her car. During the recital, one glance in her direction, and I saw tears in her eyes. Each time that I performed or sang, I would purposely locate her in the crowd and could see the joy in her tears.

Choosing to immerse myself in any music activity I could in high school kept a residual connection to my mother. I had found a temporary fix that I could engage in often that would be socially accepted. Whether I wanted to accept it or not, I was still distracting myself from addressing my emotions. I stopped verbally expressing what I was feeling and used the activities and times with friends as a distraction. In the back of my head I would be thinking, I should start to spend more time with my dad, but instead the thought that would creep up more often was, You only get four years of high school. Why not get as many experiences as possible? It was the classic angel-and-devil-on-your-shoulder scene, where the easier solution led to more consequences.

Being a part of chorus, band, musicals, and extra ensembles in addition to sports and student council activities helped me develop a new community of friends while still continuing friendships in what I would call the "Becki era." However, high school is where people branch out into preferred activities, so while I continued friendships, I was seeing less of the Becki-era friends and starting to make friends with people in grades above and below me based on the musical activities I spent more time in.

The turning point of a new era came when four soon-to-be juniors asked me a simple question in the summer before my sophomore year.

"The four of us have a band started, and we're looking for a singer. Would you want to come to one of our rehearsals to see if you are interested?" Vince, the drummer, asked.

"What type of music do you play?" I responded.

"Mostly alternative rock," he said.

I was slightly confused at how this group of guys thought I would be able to sing for an alt-rock band. I mean, my wardrobe was the classic jeans and a T-shirt style. If I ever wanted to get fancy, I would put on a flannel, plaid, or brand-name shirt. Despite my persona, I gave the rehearsal a try and by the end of the summer, we had an established name, Half Step Down, and our first backyard show.

I felt this moment had begun a new chapter in my life, which could fittingly be called the "alt-rock era." Not only was I starting to develop new friendships with my bandmates and their friend group, but also I was trying to change who I was. I viewed it as a new start and a chance to try life as an "alternative Sawyer." I tried wearing skinny jeans, I bought some Converse shoes, and I found a new persona and confidence on stage.

What was really happening through this era was me exploring my independence. Although I had already been riding to and from school on my moped, when I finally got my driver's license, I thought I had true freedom. I even started a new part-time job as a waiter, bringing in my own cash. Now, I could drive myself to school early in the morning for a music rehearsal and be home late at night after all the sports, rehearsals, and night shifts I took on. There were many days that I barely saw my dad due to our schedules, and there were often times that I went places whenever I wanted, without asking. My dad always assumed I was staying out of trouble and most of the time didn't say no even if I did ask, but this only added to the illusion that I was truly independent. I was becoming more detached from reality.

I truly valued the friendships I made during this era. However, these friends were not with me through the experience of losing my mom, and I wasn't sure if I could express my grief with them. I still had the Becki-era friends in my classes and was often invited to different parties, but I enjoyed spending more time with the new community of friends because it was something different and refreshing. Also, I personally didn't feel high school was a time that I wanted to partake in social events that involved alcohol or smoking, and this new community felt the same way. We found our own ways to be entertained such as late-night ping-pong games or a unique twist on hide and seek by using our cars to hide around our small town.

Due to not feeling as open to talking with friends, I kept my emotions bottled up until the top flew off and everything came out. I tried channeling these outbursts through my music, though. I had remembered the feeling of playing piano during my mom's funeral and how I could let emotions out without having to say a word. I could let out the pent-up emotions without hurting anyone else.

Some days I turned off the lights and played piano in the dark while I improvised what I thought I was feeling. I felt safe to cry in these moments, and this process helped me start writing songs for the first time. At the time, I wasn't receiving any "signs" from my mom, but I thought if I wrote songs about what I was feeling, I was talking to her in some way and could still be connected. I thought, People used songwriting as a way to deal with pain, right?

Being a teenager, the content of my songwriting revolved around relationships and sometimes friendships. I can smile and shake my head at the angsty lyrics I wrote during these times, but essentially, I was writing what I would have told my mom. Just how I used to talk to her about who I was developing feelings for or when she had given me words of wisdom, songwriting was the reasonable replacement.

However, as I began writing more, I began to worry that I was losing my identity in the pressure to find relationships and meaningful friendships during high school. I was most often scared to put myself out there. When I did, I felt that I was coming off as desperate to make that connection with someone. I was at a stand-still with how to cope with these high school problems because I wasn't always willing to share the songs I wrote. They were intended as a verbal communication tool, but no one truly understood what I was trying to say.

As expected, with the combination of keeping emotions in and trying so hard to start a relationship, there comes a time when things start to take a turn for the worse. Everything up until my junior year seemed to be new and exciting. I was continuing to hit milestones with music activities, even landing a lead in our school's first musical in the new, state-of-the-art auditorium. I also wasn't yet tired of the constant routine of being involved in so many activities. Junior year was when I started seeing negative effects in the "alternative" life I was living. My confidence wasn't going to be able to continue to keep things going.

The first sudden incident was hearing about Jana's cancer returning. I was afraid that history was repeating itself, and before Jana sent me the butterfly picture, I wasn't sure if my mom was with any of us through the ride. Thankfully, Jana kept the positivity and adopted the motto of "Livestrong," giving her friends and family the yellow bracelet[3] to show we all were fighters. I vowed to keep the bracelet on as a sign of my own positivity and a remembrance to my mom. Whenever I needed that motivation, I had a physical reminder.

The second incident happened shortly after Jana's news. I started to have more and more dreams about my mom and one in particular made me confused as to what it could mean. In this dream, I walked up to our house's attic to see my mom lying on the ground, possibly sick or unconscious. Two of my friends, Cortney and Jake, appeared in the attic and told me to carry her downstairs, but all I could remember was struggling to carry her. The dream was short, but I realized that the two friends in my dream were the two friends who had been at my mom's wake service and had spent time with me after the service. I had a gut feeling that the dream was supposed to be a reminder that I still had those friends. Was my mom trying to tell me that I needed to talk to them?

The third incident was the final straw that taught me an important lesson about my maladaptive coping strategies—bottled-up emotion can manifest itself into physical symptoms. Possibly through a combination of my suppressed feelings, general anxiety, and increased attempts to put myself out there relationship-wise, I finally had an anxiety attack. One simple rejection text from a girl set off a period of detachment from reality, a loss of my sense of control, the feeling of wanting to escape the situation and isolate myself, and a general weakness throughout my body.

Unfortunately, when the anxiety attack hit, I had just arrived at a cross-country meet. While the rest of my friends got ready to run, I couldn't muster the energy to get up from the ground. I had my hand above my head, lost in my thoughts, and I remember watching all the runners go by as

I had lain in the grass, emotionless. My heart kept pounding faster as my thoughts kept racing. How did I get here?

"Coach said you got sick before the race? How are you feeling now?" my friend Ryan asked as we were watching the awards ceremony.

I forget what lie I told him to continue the charade that I had become physically sick. At the same time, though, it wasn't a lie to say my health wasn't okay—my mental health, that is. Just like any other sickness, I needed to address and treat the symptoms. Instead of working on improving my immune system, I needed to find a way to fix my broken nervous system. If only I had learned as much about mental health as I did biological health in school.

The whole ride home, I was still lost in my thoughts, but I knew the time had come to talk to someone, to establish a more effective coping mechanism. When the bus arrived at the school, I headed to my car and, thanks to a simple distress text, I had a friend waiting for me there. Cortney was one of the friends in my dream, and I knew that my mom wanted me to finally open up, so why not her? We sat in my car for at least an hour as I started to realize that grief was catching up to me. I had hit a new climax in this "alt" musical and had fallen even harder into rock bottom this time.

5 "We Are Family. I've Got All My Baggage with Me."

The hardest part about additional grief is realizing that prior experience does not bring immunity from the memories and wounds being reopened.

In various movies and books, you read the same story. The main character will experience a major event in his or her life, struggle to find a way out of the situation, and slowly make his or her way through the aftermath of the event to find a happy ending. Grief is a similar story—except there is no true happy ending. Even when you have found a few, long-term coping strategies, you aren't being led to a happy ending; you are being led to a new beginning with new challenges.

It would be better to view your journey with grief as a book series that presents a new plot after you have addressed the previous. I personally like to relate my journey to the Harry Potter series,[1] for various reasons. Harry was a young boy when he learned of a new world that was forced upon him quickly and suddenly. Instead of the wizarding world, I found myself in the world of grief after spending thirteen to fourteen years in a sheltered reality. Each year of school, Harry learns more about himself and his past, and he has to face new battles that he didn't ask for. He barely has any time to process the previous year before the next year's events begin. I often wonder if we can truly call these books *fictional*.

The strongest connection I can make with Harry revolves around his actions, though. Time and time again, he pushes his friends away from helping him figure out a solution. He thought he could make sense of his past and process his experiences on his own. Each year, he repeats this thought, and each year, he is shown that the friendships and relationships that he made were in fact protecting and balancing him out. Through each additional grief, he had the constant of his friends to ground him to reality.

Sitting in my car with Cortney after my first anxiety attack was my realization that I needed to start trusting others with my emotions. First, high school alone is rough for a teenager's mental health, but to add on lingering grief from the loss of a mother makes for a strong cocktail of suppressed thoughts. Second, how could I expect to be in a romantic relationship if I didn't even express my emotions with friends? At that moment, I had spent half of high school trying to find someone else when I hadn't even found myself.

As much as I enjoyed the alternative era, I was beginning my slow ascent out of it. I still wanted to keep the friendships that I had made, but I needed to go back to who I was and be more open to myself and others. I had fell into a trap of trying to be like other friends—dressing like them, adopting their interests, and participating in their dramas. In order to step out of where I was, I needed to regain that calm feeling my mom and I had found whenever it stormed.

But after leaving the parking lot from my talk with Cortney, I was essentially returning to my storm the next day. Our rehearsals for the school musical were increasing in frequency as our show was getting closer. Beyond my own personal grief, there was a storm that had been brewing with my friends—the other cast members. There was a clear divide among certain groups, and I often found myself stuck in the middle of the issues. The issues may have started with casting assignments, but they grew into deeper issues that had always been there. I chose to step away from this battle, knowing that these types of storms come and go.

When the time came for our performances, the show was a success in many ways. We all were a part of a new age of musicals that our small town could now produce; and as expected, the euphoria of its completion was enough to clear the storm. My favorite moment of the entire experience came when Jana, now getting around by a wheelchair, greeted me after the show. She told me how proud she was of me and knew my mom was watching. In many ways, Jana reminded me of my mom and the fact that she saw me perform that night gave me a flashback to the first musical I was involved with during middle school—*The Adventures of Tom Sawyer.* That musical was the last performance my mom was able to see from me.

After the end of my junior-year musical, I realized I needed to reevaluate what was more important. It was clear to me that despite the joy that I received from all of these activities, I had forgotten to take that step back to debrief occasionally. I now had at least one friend from the Becki era who could help me learn how to be more open with my latest group of friends. I needed this reevaluation, especially as our community was about to hold a benefit event for Jana.

This event deserved my attention; it was the next plotline in my story.

* * *

One day, I received a call from Jana. At first, I wasn't sure if I should pick up because she often called my phone just to hear my mom's voice. After inheriting my mom's phone, I was afraid to change her voice mail, despite how confusing it was for people to hear when they wanted to reach me. I just wanted to hear her voice still.

Jana felt the same way and often called, saying, "Can you hang up, so I can try again for Becki's voice? I just really want to hear her right now."

I answered the phone this time. To my surprise, Jana asked if I would like to have a date at her place. I laughed at the term she used and accepted her request when she offered to buy my favorite food from the restaurant I worked at. When I arrived at her house, she was recuperating in bed, and her husband had brought the food home. Caden and Jadee were also at the house, but at a certain point, Jana wanted them to leave so she could talk to me.

Jana began to explain that the reason for our "date" was because she wanted special requests for her benefit. The first request was about dedication songs. She knew that I had created the *Becki's Songs* CD after my mom had passed, and she wanted to take a portion of her benefit event for specific songs to be played. She had me write down the songs she wanted to be dedicated to her son, daughter, and various other friends and family. She also stated that in case she wasn't feeling well that day, I was to be the one to announce all of these dedications.

Right before I left, she gave me her second request. "Sawyer, can you be there for Caden and Jadee no matter what happens? You have been through this before, and even though I've taught my children to always be positive, I know they will need someone."

"I can do that," I said as I left. I knew in that request that she had the knowledge that her time would be coming soon. Surprisingly, in my response, I knew what she was implying, and without a doubt, I knew I wanted to fulfill her request.

On the day of her benefit event, our small-town community showed the true meaning of support. The event was packed with people, auction items, performances, and matching shirts that displayed angel wings inscribed with the motto, "Livestrong." Half Step Down played a set of songs to liven up the environment, while silent auction items were bringing in numerous donations. All of Jana's extended family were present and mingling with various members of the community as they all discussed how impactful Jana has been in their lives. This event reminded me of my mom's own benefit event, but a lot bigger, and at least this time, I was actively a part of it.

The event became a party when the star herself, Jana, made her appearance. Everyone couldn't wait to talk to her and give her a hug as her sisters wheeled her around the crowd. I think the whole experience was a little overwhelming for Jana, because shortly after her entrance, she wanted to begin her address. She took center stage with a microphone and, through a labored voice, thanked everyone for showing their support. She then turned it over to me to play each song that she'd requested.

"For Caden, her adventurous son, Jana wants to dedicate 'Mama Told Me (Not to Come).'"[2] I announced. The crowd laughed and smiled as Caden stood next to his mother, enjoying their inside joke as the song played over the speakers.

"For Jadee, her favorite—and only—daughter, she dedicates 'Always Be My Baby,'"[3] I announced. The attendees of the event remained silent with tears in their eyes and their faces flowing seamlessly between a frown and smile throughout the song. However, when I announced the next song, the mood took a different direction as the whole room couldn't help but get up and dance.

"To all family and friends, Jana would like to dedicate the song 'We Are Family,'"[4] I announced. As the music started playing, there was joy on everyone's faces as they danced, laughed, and smiled. Even Jana was joining in the festivities, being wheeled around to the beat by her sisters. The event had all-around been a success.

Coming from a small-town community, the amount of presence and willingness to help a fellow community member is never short of amazing. Seeing the power of such a simple community event brought me back to the support my family had been given prior to and after my mom's death. However, I began to notice the same, immediate turnaround after experiences such as this ended. Just because the event was over didn't mean that support should stop or that the subject was taboo. If there was one thing that I learned in those first couple of years after my mom died, it was that frequent conversation and accessibility was needed for the continuation of support. I believe this was why Jana gave me her request to be there for her children.

My instinctual switch flipped on again, and I entered into a lengthy period of constant gut feelings. Jana's behavior during our "date" and after the event resembled that of my mom's as she had been declining. Both of these strong women had been preparing themselves and everyone else for what they'd already known. The wounds I had experienced anticipating my mom's death had officially reopened. Unlike with my mom where I needed a few wake-up calls to realize the signs, I felt the urge of these feelings to take action and let the emotional processing begin.

Cortney was always a great friend to consult about what was going on in my head, but now I needed to turn to some of my new community of friends that I chose to keep out of the grief conversation. Additional grief required additional support. Even Harry Potter had more than one friend to talk to. Even Harry Potter needed to gather his own army.

* * *

The first new friend I turned to was Drew. Seeing as our friendship was based around musical events, I felt that he would be willing to listen. Despite being a grade below me, he was also a part of the last performance that my mom saw of me. He most likely watched me go through my grandpa's and mom's deaths through our time in band and chorus. Not to mention, he had already been willing to share some of his own personal baggage with me. I was fortunate enough that through opening up to him, Drew became a friend who would soon be able to tell whenever something was on my mind.

"I know my time is soon," Jana said to Cortney and me. We had decided to visit her when she was placed in hospice. From her bed, she was telling us her last requests. "I want my funeral to be special, and I have some songs in mind that I want both of you to sing."

I felt as if I was having déjà vu. Similar to my mom, she wanted to make sure her funeral was special and that she had a say in the decisions. Except, this time, Jana was able to tell us in person.

"We will happily do that for you, Jana Banana," Cortney said.

I started to get another gut feeling and decided to go with it, "Jana, I have an additional song in mind if that's okay with you."

She looked at me and smiled. "I trust your judgement. Just don't forget what I asked of you. Be there for my children." I reassured her that we all would keep that promise before Cortney and I decided to leave so she could rest.

Less than a week later, I found myself waking up in the middle of the night on a Thursday morning. My dad was already up and plowing snow in town with his skid loader, waking me up with his text that confirmed that Jana had passed away that morning. I looked up from my phone and stared out my bedroom window, watching the snowfall. Yet another Thursday death.

As expected, the whole school had already heard about Jana's death when I arrived. Many people decided to wear their "Livestrong" shirts in remembrance. Also expected, Caden and Jadee were absent in order to be with their family. Everyone's mood was blunted; the atmosphere was funereal. I thought, So, *this* is what school was like when my mom died?

In our choir class, we even took the beginning to reflect on the impact Jana had made on all of us, seeing as Jadee was a fellow choir member. When the lunch bell rang after choir, Cortney and I stayed in the room. We both wanted the time to let the tears fall. I didn't feel comfortable being at school because I couldn't fully be present in my classes. I kept having a flashback to my mom's death day and how Jana had brought Caden over to my house to be with me; the simple presence of a friend had been what I needed.

Cortney and I agreed to have our parents excuse us from school in order to visit Caden and Jadee. Looking back, I am glad that I listened to what my mind needed by leaving school. Caden and Jadee were sitting at home, and although I can't speak for them, being together was helping the grieving process. We may not have talked much about Jana while we were there, but that didn't matter. I, for sure, wasn't talking about my mom when my friends and I made those silly videos the night my mom died. Henri Nouwen explained it best:

> The friend who can be silent with us in a moment of despair or confusion, who can stay with us in an hour of grief and bereavement, who can tolerate not knowing …not healing, not curing …that is a friend who cares.[5]

As the four us were talking, I looked at my phone again to a message from Drew: "R U okay?"

I smiled, thanking God that I had another friend wanting to be there for me. My grieving army had grown. I responded, letting him know that I'd decided to "visit my other family," and knew that the conversation had finally been opened enough to talk in person later. Our focus now was getting through Jana's funeral.

When my mom died, school was cancelled for the funeral, allowing those students who knew her to be able to attend. Jana's funeral, however, was set on a Sunday. Cortney and I had practiced the songs Jana had picked out for her service, and we had felt ready. I looked down at the additional sheet music in my hand as I asked a couple more friends for a request. I had stumbled upon a song entitled "Keep It Together,"[6] a couple of months before Jana's death. At one point after her benefit, I had the urge to make sheet music for this song—set for two pianos, a guitar, and percussion. The day Cortney and I met with Jana in hospice, I finally knew why I had stumbled upon this song and why I had felt the urge to make sheet music even though I had barely ever made sheet music for my own songs.

Jana's funeral service was packed full of people, stories, and heartfelt moments. Cortney and I each sang our pieces of music, and unlike my mother's funeral, I was facing the congregation. This simple change made the experience more meaningful because I was then able to have a direct view of the pulpit as Jana's husband, Dave, shared his many stories—lighthearted adventures of a spunky woman. She and my mother truly had been kindred spirits. Even the whole congregation couldn't help but chuckle as the lights mysteriously flickered during Dave's speech.

"See, even now she likes to have her own say," he said.

Dave shared many stories, but one in particular made me smile. He spoke of Jana's bond with my mother and the story of how a simple butterfly at her hospital window continued to give her hope. I looked out into the crowd in that moment and caught the gazes of my dad, sisters, Drew, and various friends from the Becki era. Their simple presence acted as a Band-Aid for the reopened wounds.

As the moment came to perform the last song, I brought in more recruits from my army: Catherine, the second piano player, who had recently become another friend who I could open up to; Cally, the percussionist, whose shared faith background gave me unending trust that we could endure; and Jake, the guitarist and fellow member of my alt-rock band who had helped me find more confidence in myself those years.

As we performed, the words "Keep It Together" resounded throughout the church and inside my own head. I felt the most emotion channeled through that song as I realized I was able to do what I should have done for my mom's funeral—sing one last time to her. This moment had become my second chance. I understood that my prior experience with grief wasn't giving me immunity from experiencing the same hurt and confusion at that time.

But I was instead able to imagine this moment as one of the iconic scenes in Harry Potter, with the entire community raising their wands in unison as they remembered all of the wisdom their fallen mentor had given them; the same wisdom that these two, strong women had taught me.[7] We could keep it together.

Perspective:

THE MOTHER

Written by Minerva Wagner

> **The hardest part about losing a child is knowing that life goes on despite saying goodbye to the life you fed, nurtured, and brought into this world.**

How do you say goodbye? It's impossible to say how you feel. The life you brought into this world, fed, and nurtured all of their life. To watch them leave you ...

Becki came into our family May of 1964 right after we finished milking our sixty head of cows on a bright sunshiny morning and in a little hurry to get to the local hospital. Her birth was quicker than her brother and sisters before her, arriving with a mop of black hair that contrasted with her pale skin. Within that same month, we took her to get baptized. When we were heading to church for her baptism, we hit a pheasant, and it smashed our windshield; glass flew everywhere. Nobody was hurt, but when we got to the church and unfolded all of Becki's blankets, there were small pieces of glass inside them. How they got inside those blankets and not hurt her is still a mystery. It was just the beginning of her eventful life.

Becki was a daredevil, an independent and smart little girl who when doing wrong would take her punishment even if it was a spanking, telling me, "That didn't hurt!" With stitches under her chin, jumping off of haystacks, and scraping her shin on machinery, she kept us on our toes, and we enjoyed watching our little caterpillar grow. She was raised in Catholic school and was a good student, with only minor incidents of talking too much in class. Being in high school presented different problems, though, with her getting a concussion from a car accident and getting herself into an abusive relationship. When she finally realized her boyfriend wasn't good for her, Bruce came into the picture, and to our joy, they eventually married.

Devastation first came into our lives in 1991 when our son, Michael, was diagnosed with CML leukemia. My husband, Paul, and I had everyone's blood tested to see who a bone marrow donor for Michael could be. Becki and my youngest daughter, LeAnne, both had good cells, but the doctors chose Becki's bone marrow instead. She donated twice for Michael, with the last donation being quite painful for her. She cried when she told me she couldn't do it again.

We all spent Thanksgiving in the hospital with Michael because the doctors had called and said that he had contracted a virus, and he wasn't doing well. To sit and watch a child of yours dying and not be able to do anything about it is painful. While Paul and our children all headed their separate ways back home, I stayed behind at the hospital in Minneapolis and went to my little room where I had been sleeping. Before I could lay down for the night, the nurses came and told me Michael had declined even more and that I needed to call the family in again.

I called everyone, but not all were able to make it back

from Iowa. I sat by Michael's bedside and held hands with him until he breathed his last. Our son was gone at the age of thirty-four. To see him wasted away to nothing but skin and bones—he looked like a skeleton. I left his room and sat down on the floor and cried. The nurses tried to console me, but I wouldn't let them help me. All the weeks I had traveled to Minneapolis twice a week to visit him as a mother, hoping there would be some help. And now it was over.

We all started home from the hospital early in the morning after collecting all of Michael's belongings. It started to snow as we drove home, and the snow got heavier the closer and closer we got to home. Becki insisted on driving me until the snow got worse, and I had to take over. When we arrived home, I only wanted to escape to my bedroom, hide away, and rest.

Making the funeral plans the next day was like walking around in a fog. I wanted to have a closed casket because I couldn't bear to have Michael shown the way he looked when he passed; I didn't realize how they could make him look like himself again. Still, we were able to view him before the wake began, and close family members were able to say goodbye one last time. You're not supposed to lose your children first, but life goes on.

I had to go back to work. I was grateful that my family at the hardware store had let me spend the last ten days with Michael. Paul kind of shut me out and didn't want to talk about Michael's death, though. So, we finally took some time off and went to visit my brother and his wife in North Carolina. Our church also offered a marriage encounter weekend that helped us deal with Michael's death. There is such a void in your life when you lose a child, but life goes on.

We planned on retiring in January 2006 until devastation hit our family again; Paul had a stroke on December 22, 2005. Becki rushed from her job at the school to get to the hospital. I prayed all the way to the hospital, hoping I could face what was lying ahead of us. The tests told us that he had a severe stroke, a bleeder in the back of his head by his neck. All the family members were there when he suddenly went unresponsive and had to have surgery. Our prayers were answered, however, as he survived. He spent many days in the hospital, and Becki was a rock to lean on as she often went with me to visit while he was still in rehab. She was even brave enough to scold her dad when he lost his temper at me.

She was too brave sometimes. She began having health problems of her own and didn't want to get help. Paul finally told her that she needed to go and see a doctor, hugging her as he said, "I've lost a child already and don't want to lose another." While we were at an appointment for Paul one day, we were surprised to find that Becki had a colonoscopy that same day. We came down a hall, and there she was with Bruce in recovery, all covered up. I told her everything would be fine, but it wasn't. Their appointment at the Mayo Clinic in Rochester proved it was the worst news—cancer of the colon. The devastation just kept piling on.

Becki called and asked me if she could come over to our house, and I went and got her. We cuddled on the couch—with me just wanting to hold and comfort her. I told her everything would be fine, and it would be all cured. All I could think about was that I wish it could have been me and not her. I even told her. Through her treatments, she kept telling me her cancer was treatable but not curable. I kept telling her that there would be a miracle.

In truth, she was getting real weak, and it was harder for her to breath. At the same time, Bruce was dealing with his father at a nursing home and Paul's brother Bob was suffering from cancer as well. Becki was a trooper, being able to make it to Bob's funeral, carrying her chemo with her. She did the same for Bruce's father five months later; but her own time had come.

When we walked into her hospital room that last night, she was on full oxygen. She motioned for me to come closer. She was anxious about the oxygen and wanted to know why we were there and where we would stay.

"I'm going to sleep in bed with you, honey," I said as she smiled a little. Paul had shut down again and wouldn't talk. He didn't want to get closer to her. He didn't want to lose another child. She wanted me to come closer again, and as I leaned down to her, she told me that she loved me.

The last thing she said to me was, "Look after my family. Help Bruce raise the kids." I said I would do the best I could before we were whisked out of the room and the fog set in again in my brain. I was wishing I had said what I'd wanted to say with her as I did with Mike, just holding his hand. I couldn't cry because I had done a lot of that in the days she was so sick. My brain just wasn't functioning.

The only thing I could think about was calling Linda, her friend from when she'd been in college in California. I realized after the fact that I shouldn't have been calling her so early in the morning, especially with the time difference. For some reason, I just had to do that, though.

We lost another child, but life went on with its many changes—both good and bad. Grandchildren got married, while Paul's health steadily declined. The church gave me the support I needed, while its school—where Becki loved to be—closed down. In 2012, I was diagnosed with non-Hodgkin's lymphoma and had to start chemo and radiation. The treatment made me lose my appetite and taste buds, causing me to lose weight; and as friends volunteered to take me to my appointments, I began to know how she felt going through those long and painful days. I luckily made it through my cancer, but I still wonder why I was allowed to be cured and not my children. That's not the way it's supposed to happen. Paul made it through his stroke despite the doctors saying only 10 percent of people live through that stroke. We both made it through, so why not our children?

I am thankful that Paul and I had each other, though. As life went on with its changes, we still had each other and had Becki's growing family near us. Even when Paul became so tired that he was falling all the time and needed to be placed in a nursing home, we had each other to accept another loss and another unwanted change. It was different not having him in our home anymore and having to make a trip to visit him each day, but life went on.

6 "Waiting on the World to Change"

The hardest part about repackaging grief is learning how to accept change in order to establish a new normal.

The interesting, but unsettling, part about grief is that although the years pass by, you'll always keep it with you as you go in some way, shape, or form. In the beginning, your baggage may come in the form of a twenty-pound trash bag that you have to carry on your shoulders; you feel as if you have to continue carrying it no matter what. You may be able to carry it for a while, but eventually the baggage interferes with your daily life, and you need the time to sit out. At some point, the baggage may become a little more manageable like a duffel bag strung over one shoulder. You can carry this weight for a substantial period, often adjusting which side takes the load, but you still feel the presence it holds—especially as more weight is shoved into that bag.

The idea that your baggage gets more compact as time

goes by is both a comforting feeling as well as a feeling of uncertainty. How am I currently handling the grief? What if my baggage gets bigger instead of smaller? When will the next switch come? The answer is that you may not know when that switch to a smaller, more portable storage container may be. At least, not until you've had the chance to look back and see how far you have come.

The size of my grief on the day my mom died was symbolically packaged in my overnight duffel bag that I uncomfortably had to fumble around with as I walked out of the hospital. On the day I had my first anxiety attack, I realized that I had allowed my baggage to upgrade in size to a bigger duffel bag. Only by beginning to open up with friends did I notice my grief load had finally gotten back to where it had begun. Jana's death showed me the early signs of resilience that I was starting to build, allowing the load to finally get smaller.

After Jana's funeral, I had moved on from wearing that duffel bag and decided to take on a backpack. Along with being a fitting choice for my high school years, the backpack resembled the support from both shoulders—my friends and family. I had at least one person to open up to whenever I needed them, and both sides were equally as comforting in managing the load. At times, I forgot the weight was even there because the new experiences and added weight made me stronger.

As with any other experience, life moves forward, though. Jana's death in the midst of mid-December made me value even more the time spent with family that Christmas. I had my dad, both of my sisters, our dog, Pyper, and even both of my sisters' dogs all in one place. Almost three years had passed since mom's death, but we still considered ourselves a family.

In those early years since my mother died, I had realized

that Christmas, along with many other holidays, felt very empty. I think in those first couple of Christmases, I was still expecting the atmosphere my mom brought to the winter season. She loved snowmen and any Santa figurines or decorations. My dad had even bought her a new Santa figurine each year to add to her abundant collection. In truth, every season was highly decorated around the house, but winter seemed to last a lot longer in our family, a possible side effect of living in the upper Midwest.

Along with decorations, my mom simply set out to make Christmas a special, memorable, and tradition-based time in many ways. Being a Catholic family, we always had the routine of going to the Christmas Eve mass, followed by spending time with my grandparents, my mom's siblings, or both, and being able to open one present of our choice before bed.

For the most part, we had our traditions, but Becki knew how to throw in some twists and turns to make each Christmas unique. Seeing as what brought her joy was being able to give her world to her family, friends, and children, she knew what truly made us happy. I often wondered why she would even ask for a Christmas list from us kids because when we opened our presents, what we received was usually an unexpected gift that we didn't even know we needed. I mean, waking up to see a huge twenty-four-pack of regular-sized white chocolate Kit Kat bars under the tree was a clever surprise. A+ for you, Mother. She's lucky I didn't give her the gift of a dentist bill after that!

She was also the queen of faking-out gifts as well. "You see that huge package underneath the tree?" she asked, pointing and smiling at me. "That one is yours."

I opened the package only to reveal a smaller package within, which eventually had clothes in it. As a child and teen, I hated receiving clothes, despite my need for them.

However, my mom's smirk wouldn't leave her face until she saw us kids look in our stockings to find that we each had received our first iPods. I can still hear her laughing and yelling, "Surprise!" That was only one of many times she used her pranks to create lasting memories.

As much as I enjoyed receiving the presents, what I learned more from my mom was her originality and passion for giving. She taught these important lessons through her actions and essentially brought the real concept of Christmas out. The holidays truly were a unique time each year with her presence.

While all of us were grieving in our own ways, we tried as a family to establish a new normal and make our Christmas season the same. The first Christmas after her death, we took a family trip to Cancun along with both of my sisters' future husbands. Despite the fact I had the flu and ended up having an interesting first-flight experience involving an air bag and an unconcerned flight attendant, we officially started the vacation on my fifteenth birthday and tried to make this experience a brand-new start.

Ever since then, we truly have gotten into a "new normal." No matter where each of us was living, we made the effort to come back to our home for Christmas Eve mass and spend Christmas morning as a family; a morning consisting of egg bakes, sticky rolls, pajamas, dogs lying on laps, watching the snowy view outside of our living room windows, and opening presents as our fireplace heated up the room. I began to look forward to Christmas because that was one of the few times we were all together.

However, the Christmas after Jana died included another addition to our "new normal." Earlier that fall, I'd started noticing my dad was spending more time with a member of my parents' card club. This member, Laurie, was a widow herself and mother of three young women; her youngest being just a grade above me and involved in many of the same school activities as me. Considering the card club consisted of a supportive community of friends, including distant family and colleagues such as Jana, I didn't think too much of my observance at first.

As I noticed my dad and Laurie's relationship more, I remember texting Emma, her youngest daughter, "Do you think my dad and your mom are dating?"

Emma responded, "I think they might? My mom did ask me if it was all right if she went on a date with your dad."

At the time, I was practicing piano, but I stopped to process that text, and I smiled. Among the chaos of our school musical, Jana's prognosis, and the many other situations that were creating discord, the thought of my dad being with Laurie made me content. Laurie had shown and continues to show how she is as sweet and caring as my mother, and I am simply thankful that my dad had found someone who shared a similar experience of losing a spouse. He was taking the time to repackage his own baggage and move forward. Wouldn't my mom want that for all of us?

Laurie became a part of my new normal and even part of the Christmas tradition. If we didn't spend time with my grandparents on Christmas Eve, we were at a party that Laurie hosted for her family. Laurie was also with us for Christmas morning, joining in on the gift-giving festivities. A change such as this—an addition to our family—could have added to my grief, but I chose to not let it. I wanted to view this change as both my dad and Laurie helping each other repackage their own grief and setting the example that we all could follow.

Thus, through these years, I started to realize that even though my mom made her unique gift-giving a highlight of the Christmas season, her emphasis on family time still happens today. Her emphasis on the giving spirit is still found among all of us, even if we often just buy what is on each other's Christmas lists. We still find ways to embrace a new normal, while keeping those long-established values in plain sight. If we needed any physical reminder of her presence during the holiday season, we could simply look at her forever-displayed Santa figurine collection in our living room.

* * *

The overall idea of "change" will always be an interesting concept for me. In a matter of seconds, you can lose someone or something, and your emotional and physical worlds are forced to change along with it. When you experience any form of grief and loss, there are immediate changes that you must come to terms with. When I was fourteen, I had to instantly tell myself, "I no longer have a mom," as well as, "I will never get to see her smile again." These were harsh realities that were forced upon me.

Author Pauline Boss wrote about learning how to live with unresolved grief. She depicted examples of families who struggle with change due to the unexpected nature of their grief, such as the loss of a loved one due to divorce or immigration, or a family member in the military who is missing in action. Are they gone forever? Are they still alive, or are they dead? These ambiguous losses can create denial, which Pauline states can be "harmful when it invalidates or renders people powerless."[1] Despite the unnaturalness of having to see my mom's body as a young teenager, I am thankful that these experiences allowed me to move past denial and move toward a healthier process of grieving that Pauline states "can begin only when the ambiguity loosens." I was fortunate, then, to be able to accept my immediate changes.

At the same time, there are changes that occur over many

years, brilliantly stated by C. S. Lewis, "Like the warming of a room or the coming of daylight. When you first notice them they have already been going on for some time."[2] Only after the years had progressed was I able to notice these longer changes, such as realizing holidays were not how they used to be and how they had adapted into a new normal. I also had noticed that each Mother's Day made me want to avoid social media due to the abundance of posts made by friends about their own mothers.

"It's funny how everyone thinks they have the greatest mother ever," my sister, Mallory, texted me one of the first Mother's Days after our mom died. I could tell that the constant influx of social media posts that day had struck a nerve with her.

I couldn't help but feel the same way. I was guilty of getting frustrated at my friends who wrote heartfelt Mother's Day posts online, directed at their mothers, some of whom didn't even have a social media account.

"Who was that post really for?" I shouted at my computer screen.

Mother's Day had finally changed for me after I went through the experience of Jana's death. I originally avoided social media and kept my mind off the subject because I didn't think I could celebrate in the holiday anymore. Jana helped me to see that there were other women in my life who had become mother-like figures and had always been there to support me. Now, when Mother's Day comes around, I happily celebrate the roles women like my grandma, my aunts, friends' mothers, Laurie, and even my sisters have had in being like mothers to me. Just like Christmas, I had found a new outlook on yet another holiday.

Still, there were bigger changes that I started to accept in my junior year of high school that became the most influential in teaching me how to repackage my grief. Those changes included how I viewed the role of music in my life as well as the importance of my faith background. Both were present when my mom was around, but they seemed more like activities that I was involved in and a simple connection to my mom rather than my identity. The change came when I started viewing them as who I am and who I wanted to be.

Getting my chance to sing at Jana's funeral empowered me, especially as I saw the effect of how simple songs can move people to tears and make them smile. On top of that, I realized that family and community members were starting to trust me more in providing music at their special events, such as memorial services, funerals, weddings, and community events. Music was initially my connection to my mom, but it seemed that I had somehow spread that connection to others through the years. The phrases "Your mom would be so proud," or, "I see your mother in your eyes," became more common to hear from people who knew my mom well.

I believe that my family was starting to, or had already recognized, the change that music made from once being my hobby to now being my identity and coping mechanism. My dad still paid for my piano lessons and even allowed me to take private percussion lessons at a university in order to prepare for competitions and auditions. My sisters bought me a simple microphone for Christmas so that I could start recording songs on my computer, which opened up new possibilities in my creativity and expression. My grandma had already taken over her daughter's duty of driving me to piano lessons, and even when I received my license, she was eager to come along with me to lessons just so she could hear me play each week. All of these gestures made me wonder if my grief was pointing me to a life's calling.

The question I found myself asking now was, "What's next? How do I embrace this change? Should I pursue music in college? Can I make a career out of music?" Luckily, I was given the opportunity to answer these questions for myself.

"Class, as we have just wrapped up another test, Mrs. Dohlman is here to lead you through a project this week before we start our next unit," Mrs. Ott, our world history teacher, explained. As our high school guidance counselor, Mrs. Dohlman took pride in her role in mentoring students through class scheduling and college preparation. Her focus for us second-semester juniors was to take the steps in researching colleges and potential areas of study.

"Your project this week is to research an area of study that you are interested in and to find programs at any school you might want to attend. You will make a poster with the information you find and will present to the class on Friday," Mrs. Dohlman explained, as she passed out the project description.

Perfect. Up until this point, I had avoided doing any real consideration of what my future was going to be like after graduation. I had always pictured myself talking this decision through with my mom, bouncing off ideas and getting her expertise on pursuing dreams considering she was brave enough to go to college in California—two thousand miles away from home. That option wasn't available now, so I took the motivation of a grade to justify doing my research. My main thought before starting my research for the project then became, "In what job can I be able to feel close to my mom every day? And, how can I be as passionate as she was with her job?"

Suddenly, I stumbled upon a program I had not heard of yet—music therapy. I was intrigued as I read through the local schools in Iowa that provided this program, and I soon found myself on the American Music Therapy Association's website, reading more about this profession.[3] Although I would soon learn much more about what the role of a music therapist meant, I understood that my relationship with music and how it helped me through the years matched the goals of this profession. I would be using music to help others in a clinical setting, providing the whole gamut of support—physical, emotional, cognitive, spiritual, and much more.

I knew that my future could still include using music for myself through writing and performing, but this new avenue of music therapy gave me that gut feeling that I learned to trust. I felt that somehow I would find my future through music therapy or through pursuing the profession. The more I thought about it, the more I could see the similarities to how passionate my mom was when working with kids in her special education classes. I had found a career option that paralleled the empathic role my mom had at the school, and even though I may not remember the grade I received on Mrs. Dohlman's project, I knew that I had learned something valuable through the process.

By embracing my newfound identity in music, I began to find there had been another change since my mom passed away. I had been naturally gravitating toward a community of people who both helped me use my musical ability and helped me find anxiety relief. This community was my church.

I grew up in a household where we attended mass on (most) Sundays. My mom kept us children active in the church community by having us be altar servers, volunteers, participate in vacation Bible school, and take religious formation classes. I will admit that I probably enjoyed these activities more for the fact that I got to be with friends. Regardless, my parents brought us up in the faith community, knowing we would be able to make our own choices of whether we wanted to make faith a part of our lives when we became adults.

During my early high school period when I was getting more involved with music activities in order to keep my mind off of negative emotions, I also joined the church's music ministry. I first joined the contemporary choir that provided music once a month at our Sunday mass. Soon, I was song leading, playing drums, playing piano, and even helping to lead music for a teen mass. What may have started as a chance to simply participate, turned into a conscious effort to stay involved and be involved as much as possible.

I also began attending mission trips every summer in high school through an organization called Catholic HEART Workcamp.[4] Our youth group traveled to a bigger city in the United States and spent a week working in the community. By day, we were providing community service, working alongside people we had just met from other youth groups. By night, we were joined together as a community of teens, young adults, and adult chaperones watching a nightly program full of music and inspirational messages. I had realized that in this week of experiences, my anxiety was gone. I wasn't being held down by my baggage. I was able to enjoy the presence of those around me, while watching the various ways each person expresses their faith. I remember looking to the staff and musicians of these camps as role models for how I wanted to show my own faith.

Through these experiences with my church community, I noticed the change in how I viewed my faith affiliation. I began to feel uneasy if I missed a Sunday mass, and I felt comfortable being there even if that meant I had to go to mass alone when my dad was out of town. Being labeled as "Catholic" or "religious" didn't necessarily bother me, whereas before I had felt embarrassed when classmates jokingly said, "Thanks for taking away the meat," to me on a Lenten Friday at school.

I acknowledged that spirituality could be another lasting coping strategy for me. I had experienced many strange coincidences with my mom's death through her butterfly effect as well as through the gut feelings that I couldn't explain. I wanted to identify as Catholic and learn more about what this specific religion believed and how grief is addressed. I thought, I wonder what the grieving process for Mary and Joseph was like after Jesus died?

Certainly, this faith could lead me to more answers, because with every religion we learned about in Mrs. Ott's world history class—Buddhism, Islam, Judaism—they all had the central belief that dying was a natural process. Mourning had to occur. Mourning had to be dealt with. I understood that religion and spirituality were not for everyone and there were many other ways to overcome grief with success. I, however, felt that my mom had given me this tool that I was finally willing to use.

I believe my affinity toward faith was the natural pull that led me to certain friends after my first anxiety attack. I often wondered why I felt more comfortable talking to certain friends, but not others. Cortney wasn't the only friend who was with me during my mom's wake, but why did I choose her to first talk to after my anxiety attack earlier that school year?

"I'll be honest. Every time that I come to your house, I swear that I see your mom sitting there on the chair in your dining room. She's always wearing that sweater she used to wear," Cortney once said, entering my house. I smiled and was excited that she was experiencing spiritual events as well and most importantly, she freely spoke about it. From that moment, we delved into a faith discussion, and I shared about my mom's butterfly effect. I knew there was a reason I felt comfortable trusting her with my emotional baggage.

As my junior year continued, I was finding similar friendships, founded in high school, that were developed through the faith community. Catherine, one of the musicians playing beside me at Jana's funeral, trusted me with her emotional baggage, especially as she went through dealing with an eating disorder later in college. Danielle, daughter of our principal and new transplant from Wisconsin, didn't even get the chance to meet my mother, but yet she said things such as, "I wish I could have met her. She sounds amazing." Both of these ladies became people I could trust, especially as we attended mission trips and various other retreats with each other.

Lastly, the friendship that I thought was built from shared musical experiences turned out to be rooted in a shared belief in faith as well.

"Thanks for letting me borrow your SD card for my phone," Drew said as he handed me back a memory chip that I slid back into my phone.

I started scrolling through my phone to find that new music files were now uploaded. I noticed a prominent Christian artist on the list and looked up, saying, "You listen to Toby Mac too?"

"Oh, sorry. I must have forgotten to delete the songs off the card, but yeah, my family listens to Christian radio. I like his stuff because he raps," Drew said.

I laughed. "Don't worry. I appreciate the new songs." I knew his family attended a different church than mine, but I never assumed whether Drew personally believed in his faith. That wasn't something you discussed at school. He clearly showed it to me, though, in the times I needed the support.

When I lost Jana's "Livestrong" bracelet one day at school, I panicked because I had not taken it off since Jana had given it to me at the start of that year. I liked having the physical connection to both her and my mom, and after realizing the bracelet wasn't on my wrist, I was anxious to retrace my steps at school.

Drew didn't question or judge my panic, so as we were waiting in the lunch line, he asked questions. "Where did you last see it? How could it have come off?" I was relieved to find the bracelet in the sleeve of a shirt I had taken off back at home, and I was more relieved that I wasn't being judged for something as trivial as a plastic armband.

Coming to terms with all of these new changes became a way for me to repackage my grief during my eventful junior year. Music and faith were beginning to ground my thoughts to the present and help me focus on the future I could make for myself. Seeing the evolution of my viewpoints in just three short years after my mom's death was remarkable, but it was also a reminder of the times I had let the grief overcome me. My baggage fluctuated and became too much for me to handle, leading to an anxiety attack. I thought I could avoid any processing and just wait for my world to change for me. However, as another April anniversary of my mom's death rolled around, I was reminded that I had more than an annual thunderstorm to calm me down now.

"Your mom is smiling down on you and proud of who you have become. Thanks for being a good friend," Drew had texted me on April 10, as I was visiting my grandparents.

I looked up from my phone, beaming, and my grandma asked, "I love to see that smile. What did that message say?"

"Nothing that I shouldn't have already been telling myself already," I answered. "I've just never received something like this on her anniversary."

"Well, it sounds like you have friends who are thinking about you," my grandma said.

More than I thought I did before, I thought. I had one more year of high school left, but with my slightly less cluttered backpack of grief, I was ready for another year.

Perspective:

THE HUSBAND

Written by Bruce Small

The hardest part about losing a spouse is knowing you will never see your life partner ever again.

To start out, I want to talk about Becki.

She always had the idea that when any time something went wrong, it would be, "That was a tumor," or "I must have cancer." I think that most of the time she was just joking, considering she was always lighthearted and full of it. But with any illness or routine checkups that she had, she always said, "Oh, it has to be a tumor!" I am sure she didn't truly believe that, but she always had an obsession with cancer. Then the ironic had to occur; she ended up getting cancer.

We first found out she had a tumor when we had to go back into the hospital to get the results of her colonoscopy. We saw her doctor and surgeon waiting in the room as we walked in, and we knew something was wrong. I think at first Becki and I were both experiencing the shock, but my feeling afterward was that we *would* beat this!

To say how I dealt with her illness, I was always thinking positive. Anytime we talked about it, I kept saying, "You are going to get through this. You will get better." I always wanted to be positive in front of her, even though deep down in the back of my mind, I always thought: What if it gets worse? What if she doesn't get better? I pushed those thoughts away to remain positive for her.

As I saw her state go downhill, the first thing I began to think about was what could I do for her? Could this cancer really kill her? I started to question my positivity and wondered what my life would be like without her; not a reality I wanted to think about. I began to look at it her through her eyes—What was she thinking? How could God put her through this? Would he take away the same woman he brought into my life?

The first time I remember seeing Becki was in our church—in God's presence. She caught my eye. She used to come into the service station I worked at to get gas and sometimes routine repairs on her car. She even used to live one block down the street from my place. Even though I knew she had another boyfriend at the time, I decided to leave a note on her car one night that said: "If you leave him, you will never regret it." I never signed that note, but luckily, she figured out who left it. We then started dating throughout her senior year in high school.

After high school, she went out to college in California to study fashion merchandising. I kept calling her for a while, but eventually she broke up with me. When she moved back to Des Moines, it was great to have her close again because we were able to get back together. We did break up a second time, but like they say: the third time is the charm! Her parents always liked me, and sometimes I felt that that was the reason why she broke up with me, because she said they liked me more than they liked her. I think she also did it just to do the opposite of what her parents wanted. Always the rebel!

I always loved Becki for her ability to do anything for anyone and the way she loved and interacted with kids. At times, though, I wasn't sure if she really knew just how much I loved her. Sometimes in our marriage, she doubted my love, asking me why I was sticking with her during her illness. I want to believe that, during her illness, she came to realize how much I really loved her and that I would do anything for her as well. I had bought her a picture frame that simply stated, "I will love you today, tomorrow, and for always." As she unwrapped her gift, we had a special moment as we began to tear up. I wanted her to know that even if she died, I would *always* love her no matter what happened, even after the years had passed.

As she continued to decline, I knew that she wouldn't have many birthdays left. We had to anticipate the possibility that we could be celebrating her last. So, we threw her a surprise birthday party at our friend's restaurant. I kept thinking, "She is going to kill me!" but I didn't care; it was all about her. We took her to the upstairs party room of the restaurant, and she was greeted by family and friends who showered her with gifts and support. I wish I could remember her reaction, but I knew she was probably mad at me. I didn't care. For once it was going to be all about her.

The night before she went to the hospital for the final time, she had a very rough night. She couldn't breathe easily and was running a temperature. The next day, I contacted her doctor's office to try to talk to her doctor, but she was busy with other patients. The doctor got back to me in the afternoon and said that we should not wait for her appointment the next day. We needed to go to the emergency room as soon as possible.

Some of our friends had already heard the news, and when I got home from work, Jana was already there with her van. Her husband, Dave, had contacted our local nurse practitioner to get an oxygen tank to take along for the ride to the Mayo Clinic in Rochester, Minnesota. They had put a mattress in the back of the van for Becki to lie down. As she put on the oxygen mask to help her breathe, she looked at me and said, "This is my friend!"

When we got to the hospital in Rochester, they took her right to the ICU unit. Through x-rays, they found that her lungs had filled up with the cancer. Quickly, I was hearing the exact same things that I had heard two weeks earlier when my dad was dying. But we had to make phone calls of our own. I contacted her sisters, her parents, and tried to figure out how to get our kids to the hospital. Soon, Becki's parents and most of my siblings had arrived due to being home for our dad's funeral.

Becki was visited by everyone, but after Mallory, Sydney, and Sawyer met with her, she became upset. She wanted to talk to me alone. She wanted me to promise that I would find a place for the kids and her parents to go to sleep. She didn't want them being around to see her in that state. It was just like her to worry more about her kids than herself. Once the kids had made it to their hotel, Becki finally felt more relaxed knowing they were taken care of.

I was out in the waiting room that morning when the hospital staff came to get me. I remember them saying, "Becki is asking for you." I went in, and it was like she was saying her goodbye. She took her last breath. I couldn't believe this was happening. I made my way to the window and looked outside, asking God, "*Why?*" How could this be? I remember just saying, "No! No! No!"

She passed away at 7:00 a.m. that Thursday morning. I remember Mallory telling me that as she was asleep at the hotel, she awoke and sat up for a reason that she didn't know. She looked at the clock that read 7:00 a.m. I believe it was Becki's way of saying goodbye to them.

When we got home, there was already a group of people at our house—taking charge and cleaning up. The support was needed, but I just remember wanting to go for a walk and get away. I needed some time to think. I let our dog, Pyper, out of her kennel—a gift given to Becki at that final birthday party—and we went for a walk. All I could think about was, What now? How can I go on? Could I finish raising our kids the way she did? How will they do this without their mother?

Becki just had such a unique relationship with our kids. I feel like she was the one to truly raise the kids and even somehow did so after her death. I noticed how fast they grew up right after she left. Mallory was already in college and the farthest away at the time. Sydney left for college after that summer, and I was surprised at how she handled all of her duties at college, becoming a speech pathologist; she normally didn't like to do things on her own. It ended up being Sawyer and me left at home. I think he had a lot to deal with entering high school, with me not knowing what to say all the time. I just tried to be there for him whenever he needed me, and I hope I did okay. Becki somehow lived on in them.

One memory that will always stick in my mind forever, though, is the day Becki asked if she would ever get to see her grandbabies. The doctor simply looked at her and shook her head no. At that point, I lost it, and I began tearing up. That was the first time that I ever let my guard down in front of her. I knew that was another breaking point for her—knowing that she wouldn't get to help her kids raise children of their own. After Becki died, Jana shared an email with me that Becki had wrote to her, telling her that exact same story—the realization that she will never get to be a grandmother.

Life did move on, though. Although I questioned my relationship with my faith in the beginning, that relationship changed over time. We always had a great faith life, but after Becki died, I questioned how much faith could still be in my life. I was able to go on a few mission trips with Sawyer as an adult leader for our parish, noticing what a great inspiration these trips had been for him and how he kept going even after I stopped chaperoning. For me, I got to see how helping other people was filling a big gap in my life. Serving others in the community and having to act as a faith mentor to these teenagers and young adults were the initiators to realizing my faith had changed. After a while, I developed the belief—and still hold onto this belief today—that someday Becki and I will meet again.

Through my grief, I—as a person—was able to move on. I would say that I dealt with my grief by staying busy through work and the company of friends and family. After everything calmed down from Becki's death, it all started to sink in. I noticed who were my close friends—the ones who made an effort to be there for me and those who have included themselves more in my life. I tried to not be alone, and if I was, I tried to have something to do to keep my mind off her being gone; but she will never be gone for me because I have my children. They have helped me deal with my grief, being a part of Becki. As long as I have them in my life, she will always be there with me.

Therefore, I was also able to move on as a widower. After a couple of years, I began a relationship with someone else. Becki had given me her blessing that I wouldn't hold on, but that I would find another person to be with after she died. I originally told her, "No. I could never," but she made me promise that I wouldn't, by choice, stay alone for the rest of my life. I can only imagine what it was like for her to express those words to me, knowing what she knew. Even in her sickness, she couldn't help but think of someone else besides herself.

I think that being in a relationship with someone else who has not only lost a spouse but also lost a spouse through the exact same thing—colon cancer—is unique. Both of us know what the other one has gone through. It's different than, say, dating someone who has been divorced; neither one of us chose to leave our spouses. We both have a greater respect for each other, and we both chose to always put our kids first. We also had been in the same friend group, and both had the support from the very same people. We know now that life is short, and you need to live it to your fullest by doing what makes you happy.

Many things may have changed in these ten years, but love has not been one of them. I changed careers, but I took the love and skills of being a mechanic with me into a related field. This new career also helped change my love of being my own boss to become a love for the lesser stress I have to deal with as someone else's employee. I'm not sure if this career change was because of her death or if this was something that would have happened eventually. Regardless, I know that I look at life differently now. I try not to take anything for granted. I try to remember that family is everything and appreciate all the friends that have stuck with me.

Do I still miss our toe-pinching, putting-others-first, beautiful butterfly? *Yes.* Do I still love her? *Yes—today, tomorrow, and for always.*

I will love you today.
tomorrow.
and for Always!

"All You Need Is Love"

The hardest part about peeling away the layers of grief is knowing that no one or nothing can truly fill the void left in its wake.

I find that random things bring back vivid memories of my mother. Certain smells, specific grocery stores or restaurants, and even movies remind me of her for various reasons. They can bring me comfort when I need it most, or they can bring down my mood depending on the memories I experience. Grief unexpectedly grabs ahold of you through these objects and places, and the memories come flooding back. Unfortunately, I don't always have control over what memories spring forward. I am at the whim of the world I live in.

Through the complexity of the brain, you are able to store memories in multiple places. In the subcortex of the brain lies the hippocampus, which stores your contextual and conscious memory. The cells of the hippocampus keep on reproducing, allowing new learning to occur each day. These memories are harder to eradicate than your working (or short-term) memory that's located in the frontal lobe, but just the same, memories in the hippocampus can still fade over time as well.

Those memories that remain clear in your mind despite the years going by are most likely consolidated in storage by the amygdala, located next to the hippocampus. These memories are described as "single trial learning" memories due to the emotional and multisensory attachment to them.[1] Studies suggest that emotional arousal can activate the amygdala, changing the memory storage process and regulating the strength of the memories in relation to the significance of the emotion.[2] Whether you experienced intense pain or extreme affection during certain moments, your amygdala may help you remember these moments for years to come.

I still have the blue tie that I wore to my grandpa's and my mom's funerals. I keep it out of sight in a keepsake box because I associate the tie with sadness. When I see the tie, grief grabs me. I remember how my mom bought the tie and how I stared at its beautiful, patterned design as I hung my head and cried while exiting the church at her funeral.

Conversely, I reexperience feelings of happiness and embarrassment whenever I hear the song "Toxic"[3] by Britney Spears. I will always remember that song coming on the radio at the exact same time each day when my mom dropped me off at school. That song was her go-to "jam" and she danced and sang in the car as my classmates stared, laughing at her personality. This song is just one of the many songs in my life that showcase the added power music has on memory storage. Music provides a cue for memory, and our emotional associations that are paired with it, by encoding them in our brain in a way that can give us an instantaneous conscious and subconscious response from simply hearing the song again.[4]

Thus, in some cases, music could be the most powerful and negative trigger for someone's grief.

In an odd pairing of emotions and memories, though, I associate the movie *Shrek*, Valentine's Day, and my mom together. Why? Simply because I have the unique memory of my mom on Valentine's Day having me walk into our laundry room and look under a pile of dirty clothes in order for me to find a "surprise" in the midst of the messiness. I had learned to trust her bizarre requests by then, and so I searched through the laundry to find her gift. I pulled out a VHS copy of *Shrek* and heard my mom say, "Happy Valentine's Day!

"Now, don't tell your sisters or your dad I got you a gift. I knew you liked that movie, and I couldn't help from buying it," my mom said, smiling. Although I didn't tell my sisters about my mom's special gift, I had a strong suspicion that she had also bought something for them as well. She just wanted to make each of us feel that we were special.

I still enjoy watching that movie today, especially because of the vintage VHS tape and dirty laundry that I picture in my head thanks to my mom's "secret" Valentine's Day gesture. However, I enjoy the movie today because I've realized that the main character in that movie, Shrek, describes another perfect metaphor that I feel also applies to a journey with grief. He stated that ogres are like onions—they have layers.[5] In order to get to the core, you have to peel through the many outer layers that are protecting what's inside.

In my own process of repackaging my grief, I had to address the new issues that came with each year, situation, event, or any new change. These issues were essentially my layers of grief that had been placed on me ever since my mom died. I had the choice of leaving these layers on, keeping up my defense mechanisms, and being numb to any emotional situation that happened to me, or I could slowly make my way through the layers to make my grief load smaller.

The movie jokes about Shrek's use of an onion to describe the idea of layers. Why couldn't he have stated something else that has layers, such as a cake or parfait? Considering I am an avid fan of tacos, why wouldn't I decide to view my grief as a 7-layer taco dip? Plain and simple—just like onions, grief stinks!

My mom wouldn't want me to continue to let grief be a burden on me or my family. She would want me to move forward with my life and learn how to cope with all of these changes. After three years and one anxiety attack later, I had learned that I was better off peeling these layers of grief away in order for me to make progress in my journey.

The next layer of grief that I was facing was my anxiety over relationships. I am still intrigued at how I could be both so scared of and yearn for a close personal connection with a girl. As I was about to be entering my senior year of high school, I had not dated anyone in my high school career, but there were many times I desperately wanted to. I had let the drama of dating be one of the catalysts in my high school anxiety breakdown and had most likely caused the same effect on other girls who were brave enough to disclose their feelings toward me, only to have me not give them a chance due to my fear of a commitment.

I was just so puzzled as to how the idea of dating changed so quickly after my mom died. In middle school, I was very confident and experienced my first relationship, breakup, and subsequent relationships. Embarrassingly, my "confidence" and middle school naïveté meant that within those three short years, I had dated three different girls and got back together with two of them multiple times.

These middle school relationships may have only been the hand-holding-at-movies and awkward-slow-dancing-at-dances type of relationships, but I still experienced heartbreak when they ended. My mom was the person who helped me develop my emotional maturity through those years. She coached me through how to get over my first experience being broken up with and wouldn't hold back her thoughts on the idea of me getting back together with an ex. "If it didn't work the first two times, why go through it again?" she said.

Her support stemmed all the way back to elementary school when she kept an eye on who I sat next to during lunch to see who my latest "crush" was. She may have gone too far with her "support" at times, though.

"So, my mom told me that your mom said you like me and Alexa," Jenna, a fellow second grader, said one day at school. I am fairly certain I remained quiet during that awkward lunch. I am also fairly certain that I wasn't quiet after school when talking to my mom about my thoughts on her actions. Again, thanks to the extreme emotions of embarrassment and anger, I can still relive that awkward memory for many years to come.

Overall, despite her nosiness, I appreciated my mom's advice and valued her input in developing my maturity in the world of relationships. She was the first person I could talk to about who I developed feelings for and how I could get the courage to ask that person out. After her death, I no longer had her input. I no longer had my confidence. What I had been reading about was true: trauma doesn't just cause your mood to change; it can also cause self-doubt.[6]

I no longer had that input or confidence because I was unwilling to talk about this subject with anyone else, including my sisters. Leading into my senior year, both of my sisters were engaged to be married. They both had been dating their fiancés for over four years and started their relationships in high school. More importantly, both of their fiancés had gotten to know my mom before she'd died, and she'd given her blessings to both couples. As their weddings approached that year, I felt like the outcast of the family, and I yearned for a similar emotional connection. I needed to fill the emptiness left in my mom's wake, even if the filler was supposititious.

"Dude, she likes you, and she has already become a part of the friend group. Why don't you date her already?" my friend Josh asked.

He was talking about Jayme, the younger sister of one of our friends. Jayme—the same girl who had admitted to her friends her crush on me the previous year. Josh was right. She had already expressed that she liked me, and she had been coming to some of our get-togethers that previous year. She also had been my date for my first high school prom. Better yet, she even was best friends with Jana's daughter, Jadee, so she had gone through the same experience of losing someone who was like a second mother.

As much as it all made sense to act on Josh's suggestion, I felt physically sick to my stomach at even the thought about a relationship. If someone even joked about me dating Jayme, or anyone else for that matter, my heart pounded faster, and my mind began to go into anxiety mode. I soon became numb to my emotions. It was as if grief had found a new way to pull me in through the abstract terms: dating and relationships. Previous rejections and burnt-out confidence made me not want to think about those words. I couldn't tell if I was too scared to accept something that made sense or if I truly didn't have feelings for this younger girl.

I started to ignore the comments from my friends and simply began to focus on my last year of school as well as the close friendships I had been making. Jayme had become a good friend who wasn't just a part of our group, though. She was someone who would listen to my problems. I promised myself to be more open with other people in order for me not to have anxiety meltdowns again, and Jayme was becoming one of these go-to people. It was easier to talk to someone a couple grades younger because any input from her was an outsider view. Additionally, I didn't have to worry about her pressuring me into a relationship like everyone else did.

The downfall of me being open and honest with Jayme was that it fueled the comments and pressure from our friends for her and me to date. Jayme and I had a closer friendship than before, and the pressure made me think about the reasons why we had become closer. Did I develop feelings for her somewhere in the numbness? Am I just holding myself back from any commitment because I'm too afraid of losing another close friendship?

I didn't know the answer to these questions, but I eventually decided to go with one: I had developed feelings for her. Maybe if I accepted it, then that feeling in my stomach would go away, and I would be surprised at the emotions I was capable of. I was beginning to accept the idea of a relationship, and I remember feeling liberated from my clouded mind. I was taking a step forward—I was peeling away a layer of my hardened exterior!

That first step started the day that I admitted to Jayme that I had the same feelings for her that she did for me. We had just gone to see a concert with friends, and by the time we came back, there was a budding secret between us. However, like most secrets, it didn't last long. Within a day, her friends already knew, and the gossip made its way to my friends.

"So ... you and Jayme are officially talking, huh?" Drew said as we got done with another run during summer cross-country camp. I tried to play it off as if I didn't hear him or know what he was talking about. "That means we can go on double dates!" he added. I just smiled and accepted that I would be getting similar comments more often once school started.

With school starting, the gossip had already spread far, and it had become reality. I decided to accept that reality and realize that although I didn't have my mom with me every step of the way in this last lap of high school, I, at least, had someone else by my side as I reached for my goals. Goals that included finally making it into the Iowa All-State Music Festival after getting as close as the first alternate for instrumental percussion in that previous year. Goals that included being there and writing songs for both of my sister's weddings that year. Not to mention, I had the looming responsibilities of needing to finally finish my Eagle Scout project and audition into my favorite university's school of music before the first semester ended. Thank, God, I have someone by my side, I thought again.

My goals were daunting, but I was willing to work for each one. I felt the momentum of the new school year and excitement of a potential girlfriend both pushing me to turn a new chapter in my life. I was practicing music more thoroughly, taking additional private lessons, planning the grunt work for my Eagle Scout documentary project, and planning my last year as best as I could. It helped to have someone as a personal cheerleader to motivate me through it all.

"You are going to be so prepared for the All-State audition. This is your year to make it—I just know it!" Jayme said.

"I can only hope so," I responded. I knew that making it into the All-State Music Festival would be a tribute to all of the time and money my mom spent cultivating my passion for music.

"Don't worry. After October 22, you'll officially be an all-stater!" she said, gleefully.

I remember admiring how confident Jayme was about herself and other people. If only I could steal that confidence. Even if she was self-conscious, she put on an assured persona. I thought, October 22, that's getting close. She's right, though. I'll be prepared by then!

My heart started pounding as a realization hit me in that

moment. The last weekend in October had always been All-State auditions, but why had this date all of a sudden seemed even more familiar than usual? It had finally hit me—my oldest sister, Mallory, had set her wedding for that day! Why had I not put the pieces together up until that point? What was I supposed to do?

The process of telling my sister the dilemma I was facing went as expected. She was upset that I would even consider the situation a choice. I was supposed to be an usher in the wedding and had even been asked to write a song for her and her fiancé, Matt. At the same time, I thought I needed to finally make All-State to prove to myself music was my calling. What would Mom have said in this situation? If I made All-State, would she still be proud even if it meant missing my own sister's wedding?

Before the stress of the situation could get to me, Mallory said, "Fine. Go to your audition, but I want you there for the reception to play our first dance." In her voice, I could still hear how upset she was and that she was hoping I would change my mind. Unfortunately, my mind was set on making my goal. I had to prove to myself I could do it; whatever "it" had become.

"Just imagine, when you finally get into All-State, you can arrive at your sister's reception in style!" Jayme said, winking.

"I think you mean both of us will be arriving in style," I added. She looked at me with a questioning look. "I'm allowed a plus one. Would you like to come?"

Jayme smiled brightly, "Of course!"

At that point, we had already gotten closer, and my family had known about me "talking" to someone. I was trying my best to move forward and finally let someone into my life. Or, more importantly, I was finally letting someone into the two most guarded parts of myself—my head and my heart. The time was coming when I needed to just strip off that layer of protection on my grief and see what lay underneath.

I decided to take the final step and officially ask Jayme to be my girlfriend during homecoming. The moment I did, I knew I had come a long way from the fourteen-year-old who'd lost his emotional crutch. On top of celebrating the successes of high school thus far, my senior-year homecoming made me look forward to the rest of my school career. I hadn't had an anxiety attack for a year, I had just been accepted into the university of my choice, and I now had a girlfriend. I was back on top of the world!

You could say that the memories of that homecoming were heavily influenced by my amygdala. Strong, powerful emotions that I experienced in that one week left a lasting impression in my brain. You could say that most of my grief journey has left vivid memories just like homecoming week. However, the arrival of October 22 gave me another lasting scene to share.

"Keep me up to date with what's going on at auditions. Lori will be picking you up as soon as you are done to bring you and Jayme to the reception. Good luck!" my dad said as I left for my last year of All-State auditions.

"I don't think I'll need it. I have a good feeling about today," I responded.

I had an odd confidence going into that day. I wasn't sure where the confidence was coming from, but I began to embrace what was coming naturally. *So, this must be how Jayme feels every day,* I thought. I must had been learning to adopt her positive attitude in that short month that we had already been dating.

Arriving at the auditions, I felt ready to take on the challenge. I had attended auditions the previous three years and knew the routine for both vocal and instrumental auditions. In order for me to obtain a spot in the All-State

Band, I needed to score enough to make a recall audition and then score higher than the thirty-plus other percussionists fighting for the two open spots. "I got this," I said to Jayme.

The day went by fast. I went in for my first audition and played just like I had practiced a million times. I waited for the first results to find that I had made a recall audition! More waiting ensued, and I finally was able to do my recall audition. I left the room feeling tremendous, and I knew the odds were favorable with the two spots being narrowed down to five people.

Now, the moment I had been waiting for had finally come. The school volunteer came into the gymnasium with the roll of paper that would be posted on the wall for the results. The volunteer made her way up the ladder, moving as slow as ever. She stuck the piece of paper to the wall, and I stood there with Jayme as we both watched the paper roll down to reveal:

First Alternate: Sawyer Small

Immediately, I hung my head and tears fell down my face. The loss of a childhood dream. Instantaneously, I felt someone hugging me, and my phone buzz with messages. I didn't want to read them, nor did I want to speak. I just wanted to exit the building as soon as I could.

In what felt like a few seconds time, my mom's friend, Lori, found me and Jayme to take us to my sister's wedding reception. I still couldn't speak and was trying to slowly get my mind off of the dream that was just shattered. Stop these tears. You need to put on a game face when you walk in. Don't ruin Mallory's wedding, I kept telling myself over and over in my head. Jayme and Lori were trying to talk to me throughout the car ride, but my mind wasn't ready to speak.

I felt like I had just taken a step back from the confidence I thought I had.

We arrived at the wedding, finally. I didn't even bother to put on my suit jacket. We entered the ballroom, and I noticed that the wedding party was already at their head table, and food was already being served. As Jayme and I were being led to our tables, I felt like everyone's eyes were on me. I assumed they were probably wondering why I was such a terrible brother for missing my own sister's wedding or why I look so depressed on such a joyous occasion.

"How did you do?" a fellow classmate asked as I passed by. I looked at him, shook my head no, and the tears began to pour again.

As I sat down, I looked up at Mallory at the head table, and I felt ashamed. Seeing her in her white dress made me regret the decision to chase after a pointless accolade that wouldn't truly define who I was as a musician or person. The audition was meaningless. I now will always have to live with the memory of abandoning a family member. So much for putting family first. I now have to live with more objects and events that pull me into negative emotions. Mom would have been ashamed of my actions, I thought.

"Hey Bean," I heard Mallory say as I looked up from hanging my head down to see her right next to me. Her usage of my childhood nickname cued me that she was trying to comfort me. "I heard what happened, and I want you to know that I love you. You are an amazing musician. You know that mom would have been proud no matter what, right?"

"But I missed your wedding. I'm a terrible brother. I should have taken it as a sign when I found out they were on the same day," I said.

"All that matters is that you are here now. I've been looking forward to hearing the song you wrote for Matt's and my first dance. Can you still do that?" she asked. I looked at her and nodded yes. I needed to do that for her and Matt.

As the time came for the first dance, Matt and Mallory made their way to the dance floor as I made my way to my keyboard which was set up to the side of the dance floor. I brought out the lyrics to the song I had recently written for their big day. I sat down at the piano bench and looked out in the crowd to my family once again. I noticed their eyes fixed on me and the newlyweds. I saw the reassuring smile on Jayme's face.

I knew in my head that I had just opened a new layer of grief that day, and I would never forget it. In the words of Charlie Walton, grief is a "never-ending process of coping" and "there are some wounds that time can never heal."[7] I had tried to fill the void of this recent layer with whatever I could, but I was unsuccessful. Maybe the void could never be filled, and time would not ever fix that. Maybe I just needed to continue this never-ending process to learn how to accept the emptiness of the latest layer. So, I took a deep breath before doing what I knew best to cope: performing from the heart.

All we said is talk is cheap
All we have is a love that's deep
With it said and done, we've said it all
All we bring is used in time
All we leave is left behind
With it said and done, we've said it all[8]

Perspective

THE DAUGHTERS (PART TWO)

Written by Mallory Nicholson

> **The hardest part about losing your mother, is finding your life's calling without the parent who made her family *her* life's calling.**

I wasn't sure what to think about God anymore. I wasn't even sure what to think about the world we lived in. My two friends, Meaghan and Alyssa, came over to our house that weekend after she passed. I told them, "I don't understand how God could do this. There are killers and murderers living in this world, and even if they are caught, their families can still see them or talk to them." For a while there, I honestly didn't know how to feel about religion as a whole.

I wouldn't say that I'm an extrovert, but I also can't say that I'm an introvert; it depends on the situation. But I quickly became an introvert immediately after her death and continued feeling that way for a couple of years. From what I've observed with my siblings and myself, we all withdrew in ways. We were barely ever "partiers" or felt the need to go out to bars in college. I think a lot about this withdrawal and wondered if this was just who we were as people or if we changed because of our mom's death. Were we always destined to be introverts and more reserved, or was that personality forced on us by events?

I stayed home on weekends during college and studied, just like on the days I received those phone calls. I was very lonely. I wouldn't say depressed, but I withdrew from a lot of people. Matt was four hours away from me at a different college, and I felt like I had no one. I wasn't close to anybody and didn't feel like I had any attachments. I was making more friends and was closer with the people at Matt's college because I traveled to see him more often. I may have liked where I went to school, but at the same time, I didn't; it was a lonely place. I hated how I had to return to this lonely place the day after her funeral and take a test. None of that stops. The world makes you keep going.

I became very wishy-washy with what I wanted to do in life. I sometimes think that my mom's death made me more confused about what I wanted to do and what I wanted to be. I normally talked to my mom about those decisions. I kept thinking about wanting to go into nursing, but never pursued that route. Even after switching from psychology to biology, I still was unclear where my mind and heart were at.

I eventually became intrigued with nutrition and being a dietician. I became more invested in dietetics when I finally had an internship in a hospital, working with people who had cancer. I got joy out of helping patients who had cancer, imagining if I could have done something similar to help when my mom was sick. However, I couldn't have helped. I'm glad I was naïve to the situation when I was younger because I couldn't have saved her.

During my time trying to decide what I wanted to do, it made me want to be a mother. I worked as a dietician for a few years, but my heart was in a different role. My mom had a job, but at the same time, I wouldn't have considered her a profession-oriented woman who put her job first. She wasn't a stay-at-home mom either, but she was always there for us. She had a lot of time off around our schedules and made our schedules hers—even keeping a personal planner that was filled more with our events than with her own commitments. I think I always knew, but after she died, it solidified the fact that a job is a job, while family is a career.

Within three years of her death, I began my family and got married. A huge time in anyone's life is his or her wedding, but mine was hard, and I don't remember as much as I would like to about it for some reason. I was jealous of other women's relationships with their mothers, especially during their wedding planning and wedding day because I didn't have that; I just had Matt's mother.

However, I do remember saying to Matt: "I honestly can't imagine marrying someone else. For me to tell someone else about you and how you were by my side in some of my worst times would be too difficult for me and for that person." Matt truly was with me throughout my grief. He kept me from my loneliness. I can't say for sure, but her death brought us closer. I imagine we still would have gotten married regardless, but it's still an interesting thought that our paths could have changed if she were still alive.

When I finally had my first child, her death hit me again. I thought her absence during my wedding was hard, but when I had my first boy, Landry, I am positive I had some type of postpartum depression. I had high emotions that changed at the drop of a pin, I felt overwhelmed and tired, and I didn't have anyone there to call. "Mom is this normal? Landry's running a temp—what do I do?" I couldn't share these moments and ask for her to help with the many firsts of raising a child. I wanted to go back to the days when I would lie down next to my mom and talk, never wanting to leave the warmth of the bed. In those many talks, we even talked about the idea of me having a child. She once said, "I can't wait to see you have a girl. One with lots of hair just like when you were born."

My firstborn was the exact opposite, but I still didn't stop me from breaking down and crying, remembering how sad she was when she realized she wouldn't get to see her grandchildren—let alone my shaggy girl. Then, came our second baby boy, Lincoln. Looks like you'll have to wait a little longer for that girl, Mom. Sometimes when Landry was little, he just sat on the floor and looked at the ceiling or corner of the room, and I thought, What are you doing, child? In my head, I wondered if that was her talking to her grandchild; I want to believe it was her, at least.

On her ten-year anniversary, I will have been a mother for three and a half years. My kids are truly my career as a stay-at-home mother. What's important to me is shaping my kids and being more of a mother figure, something that keeps me connected to her. Yet I'm finally understanding how much strength it took for my mom to be able to leave us kids. You don't realize how much strength it takes until you are in that role, trying to imagine what it would be like if the same happened to you. Even worse, you imagine the strength you would need to deal with the grief of losing your own children to any circumstance.

I may have learned to deal with the trauma of losing a mom and have come to terms with the grief of losing the older members of our extended family, but I am not free from future grief. Before something happens, you think it's the worst thing that can happen to you. For that, I'm not scared of the types of loss I've already experienced because I imagined they would be the hardest things I would have to deal with. I felt I almost became numb over watching people who are older die due to working in that environment and the fact that there's often a sense of relief from the caretakers and family who are glad their loved one is no longer suffering. However, I now know that there *is*, in fact, grief that can still hit as hard or hit worse than what I've already experienced. I now have so much anxiety over what could happen to my kids and I can't imagine what it would be like to lose them; a new layer of grief I had not expected.

What helps me deal with the stress and anxiety is to continue living like my mother—at least, the positive traits that still stick with me. Every year, I forget more and more different things, but what I do remember is how she didn't take life so seriously. She entered rooms, singing at the top of her lungs in what I liked to call a "karaoke voice." You know—the voice that's good enough for karaoke but "you're-clearly-not-a-singer" voice. My two little boys now have to deal with me breaking out into spontaneous opera with my own "karaoke voice." Matt also has to deal with me doing whatever I can to annoy him thanks to my mom's relationship with my dad. Furthermore, I've even adopted her obsession with change by constantly rearranging our household décor just like that quirky woman who raised me.

Change has been a common theme in this past decade. As Sawyer has written, our family has had to accept many changes, both good and bad. I have mixed feelings about the changed relationship I have with my siblings because I wonder if we would have spent more time with each other and if we would have come home more often if my mom had still been around. I know at least Sydney, my mom, and I would be doing more girls' weekends. I think that's why I try to FaceTime Syd as often as I can.

Further change, I never imagined the idea of having a stepmom or stepsiblings or having a blended family. I never imagined my mother passing, either, but I remember thinking, it couldn't have been a more perfect person for my dad to date. Going through similar experiences, neither one of them has to feel guilty or feel ashamed about talking about their loved ones. They feel comfortable because they can talk about their past lives. I'll admit, the first time Landry called Laurie "Grandma," it hit me then too; but, if my own son can accept the reality we have now, I can as well.

Grief overall changes your outlook on life. You just don't waste time. I feel like my siblings and I had to emotionally grow up faster than normal and begin the next parts of our lives. There are still times when I look at Sydney and think, You are way too grown up for your age. Life simply jumps forward, and soon enough, you're ready to be writing about the initial grief that happened a decade ago.

What I've learned about grief is that the journey is very cyclical, up and then down. It has tested my faith—one day feeling everything is okay and the next day breaking down. With grief, it's never a high "high," but it's a new normal that you live with—even when it hits you again and turns into a sad day. I obviously grieve for my mom to be here, but I feel like I've stopped that big grief cycle I used to be on. The longing is still there and won't fully go away, but time has given me a new perspective that has helped me to not be weighed down by the grief.

What does weigh on my heart is knowing that someday I may finally have a daughter. It will be my mom sending me a signal, saying, "Here's your girl. She has lots of hair, just like I promised." That day will pull me further into that longing, and I may realize I'm still in that cycle; but for now, I have my boys to calm my heart.

"That's you, Mom. And that's *your* mom," Landry says as he points to a photo of my mother, sister, and me. "That's the mom in heaven," he adds, smiling at me. It makes my heart pitter-patter. I love my career.

8 "In the Cycle, the Cycles of Life"

The hardest part about the cycles of grief is convincing yourself to take that step forward when you experience a setback.

Experiencing symptoms of grief can be a cyclical journey. I've come to learn that in one moment, you can be riding a natural high from positive life events, and the next moment your emotions can be pummeling down in the opposite direction. Grief acts like a roller coaster, taking us on a ride through unexpected twists and turns. No matter how many times you experience a roller coaster, you will still endure the push and pull of the ride that gives you that gut-rising feeling in your stomach and chest.

Unlike most roller coasters, however, you are not able to see what is coming next with grief. Sometimes you don't recognize which cycle you are in until you can look back and notice the change in attitude or emotions that you had. Was I truly on an upward climb in this mountain of grief, or was

I still stuck where I was before, grasping at what I thought were sturdy rocks? Other times, you are fully aware of which cycle you are in, having felt the euphoria of reaching the next plateau or felt the depression you made in your surroundings from the downward fall.

Prior to Mallory's wedding, I knew that I was riding upward. I had just reached a new height in my ability to cope, which showed in the confidence I was regaining. I was willing to let my guard down but failed to prepare myself for possible failure. Thus, when I watched one of my high school dreams shatter before me, a veil was lifted again, and I realized that I had forgotten the importance of being there for my family in their own personal milestones.

Milestones came in all sizes, and my mom stressed the importance of being there for any and every. Some of my earliest memories are of me being dragged to every sporting and school event of my sisters. This is typical of many younger siblings, but I still understood the importance. I had watched my sisters play softball so much that when it came time for me to play T-ball, I had adopted their left-handed swing and confused my coaches when I threw the ball with my right, dominant hand. On the other hand (pun intended), my mom made my sisters attend my events as well, despite their busier, high school schedules. She simply wanted our family to be together.

Therefore, the day after Mallory's wedding consisted of me not leaving our living room couch. I had my own personal pity party over not getting what I'd wanted and missing out on a significant family event. At the same time, I was reliving the previous day over and over again in my head—seeing my sister in her dress for the first time and thinking how stunning she looked on her big day. I continued to admire how beautifully she had designed her reception; a space that reminded me of my mom's eye for fashion and decorating.

I was reliving the conversation I'd had with Mallory after I'd arrived at the reception. She spoke to me in a way such as my mom did when I experienced hardships, like a breakup. I could see the compassion in her eyes and felt her caring from a simple hug. Once again, I realized that my sister had naturally stepped into a motherly role. She could have expressed anger or even said the clichéd, "I told you so," or, "You should have listened to me," but just like my mom, she was able to forgive in a heartbeat. She put others before herself.

I didn't stay at the reception too much longer after the first few dances. I remember trying to force myself to dance to the usual upbeat music at weddings, especially because Jayme wanted to cheer me up. I thought perhaps, if I let loose, I would enjoy the celebration and forget the first half of the day.

Looking back at the pictures of the reception, though, I could see the depressed look in my dulled eyes and fake smile. I just wanted to go to the hotel room, go to sleep, and hopefully wake up from yet another nightmare. So as I relived these memories that next day and returned to school that week, I had entered a depressed cycle in my grief journey.

I had skipped lunch the first day, and I, instead, talked to my choir and piano teacher after class. No matter what they were trying to say to reassure me that my passion for music was still there, I was failing to see it. Jayme even came back from lunch to bring me a sandwich so I wouldn't go without eating, but even her positive energy wasn't enough to bring me back up to my confidence.

It didn't take long for my blunted demeanor to affect those around me as well: "Are you mad at me?" Jayme asked.

"No, I just don't feel like talking right now," I replied. I truly wasn't mad at her, but due to my negative mind-set, I began to feel a little annoyed that she would ask me that question considering the fact that she had been there during the auditions and the wedding. She'd seen what I'd gone through. I'd just lost an important dream of mine! Wouldn't she understand that I just needed some time to get over it? Well, *now* I'm mad! I thought.

Despite having told her I wasn't upset with her, I began to understand that actions spoke louder than words—especially in a relationship. I soon received a text from Jadee that said, "Why are you mad at Jayme? She is in class, crying. She says you won't talk to her."

I looked at my phone and became angry. I had talked to her! This isn't about her. I'm just upset with myself! I shouted in my head. Now, even having a girlfriend wasn't helping me control my emotions. I began to wonder if I had made a mistake getting into a relationship. I had wanted one all throughout high school, and at that point, I questioned if I jumped into one too soon.

Like any other situation, I had been able to calm down, talk to Jayme, and vaguely explain why I was acting weird. However, after that, I began to stay at home and go to work more often. I didn't have the motivation to hang out with friends, and even if I spent time with Jayme, I was lethargic. She brought over pumpkins to carve at my place on Halloween, but instead I wanted to lie on the ground, and I never even touched the pumpkins. I could tell she was upset, and I even remember hearing her friends tell this exact story a couple months later.

I decided to not participate in basketball season that year, as well, despite having played every year since youth league. I enjoyed basketball ever since my dad had taught me how to shoot a ball and trained me for free-throw competitions. Nonetheless, I chose to sit out my senior year with the excuse that I wanted to pick up more hours at the restaurant I worked at in order to save up for college. I also used the excuse that I needed to finish my Eagle Scout project before my eighteenth birthday in December. I was lying to myself, though. If I'd wanted to, I could have juggled all of those activities easily. I was just looking for a way to isolate.

In some odd way, I think I needed to spend more time at home, though. I needed to slow down from all of the activities I was involved in so that I could actually address what was going on in my head. Perhaps my depressed mood was nature's way of shutting down my nervous system in order for me to adapt to new events that I couldn't handle.[1] Being at home grounded my thoughts with its sense of security, lifelong memories, and even a dog that acted as my minitherapist. Pyper was always by either my dad's or my side when we were home, just like she had been for my mom throughout her treatment.

For as much as I felt that Pyper was consoling me, I knew that my dad and I were consoling her as well. When my mom died, Pyper's behavior had changed. Whenever anyone left the house, she barked uncontrollably and whined when she was put in her kennel. Each time she did this barking fit, I remembered her doing the same when my mom had walked out the door her last time.

After a few years, Pyper began to have seizures that caused her to collapse on the ground and shake. She took long, raspy breaths with her jaw wide open. These spells lasted a few minutes before she was able to get up again. The vet had explained that she was experiencing a blockage of fluid, or hydrocephalus, in her brain that was possible—but not common—for a Cavalier King Charles cocker spaniel.

During some of her seizures, I wondered if she would ever come out of them. My heart stopped as I watched her shake, become stiff at moments, and drool from her mouth. Her eyes would roll back into her head. Sometimes, I held and petted her until the seizure was over, the least I could do for the dog that was always by my mom's side.

Finally, the day came. On Thanksgiving of my senior year, my dad walked into the living room as I was working on editing my Eagle Scout video project. I took my headphones out to hear what he was saying.

"Pyper took her last breath. I don't know if you want to go and say your goodbyes. She's lying in the laundry room," my dad said slowly. I knew in his voice that he had a hard time getting that statement out.

Pyper was lying on the ground, motionless as I walked in the laundry room to see her. I got down on my knees and petted her one last time. I didn't know what to say or feel in that moment, except that I was relieved she wouldn't have to suffer through those seizures anymore. She wouldn't have to suffer at all.

We may have only had Pyper in our lives for four years, but I felt that she had been a part of our family my whole life. I remember hearing her first bark one summer night as my mom and I were sitting outside admiring the storm clouds. She went with my dad and me every morning when we did our paper route. Most importantly, she gave us the joy we needed each and every day we had her.

As my dad took her to the vet and set up the plans to have her cremated, I began to put my mind back into place. In those four years, this dog had spent her whole life comforting and bringing joy to a family. Even in her short time, she took on the role of being my mom's emotional support dog. With Pyper's passing, I could have viewed it as losing one of the last few connections I had to my mom, but I didn't want to. I wanted to imagine her being reunited finally with my mom in the afterlife, running and jumping into her arms with her soft, floppy ears.

My aunt, LeAnne, said it best one day when she said, "I honestly believe that Pyper was put on the earth for one reason—to be of comfort to Becki and you all during this time. I think that Pyper's death, not long after Becki's, is further proof that she had accomplished what God intended and it was her time to join your mom."

The Thanksgiving that Pyper died was another wake-up call. I didn't want to continue my pity party for myself. I didn't want my negativity and demeanor to affect other people in my life. I needed to find that positivity I had felt before so that I could be motivated to finish out my senior year. As Sheryl Sandberg wrote in her 2017 book about finding resilience, *Option B*, "In the wake of the most crushing blows, people can find greater strength and deeper meaning."[2] On that holiday, I was relearning to appreciate what I still had and recognizing that the grief baggage wouldn't be able to weigh me down if I used these obstacles and setbacks to make me stronger.

* * *

A conclusion I had come to through these years was that I was able to take charge of my grief if I wanted to. When we face an obstacle in life, we have a few options: we can let the negative event take control of our thoughts, emotions, and actions, or we can take action to control our thoughts, emotions, and the event itself. Losing Pyper was an early example of myself refusing to let yet another natural life event affect my behavior. In honesty, taking action after loss of any kind is not easy, but I was willing to take any step that wasn't backward.

My first step was to focus on my Eagle Scout project. The project completion was the last barrier I needed to cross in the long road I had been a part of through Boy Scouts.[3] I wouldn't consider myself a very outdoorsy person or someone who likes to do the stereotypical Boy Scout woodworking or hunting, but I valued the life lessons I had learned in the organization. I spent years in meetings, camps, merit badge colleges, and various events that would help teach problem solving skills and help me to increase my ranking in the organization. Now, I was using one of the life skills I had been taught, and I was taking ownership for my own well-being and for my project, a project that commemorated the history, current affairs, and future of my church.

My project was essentially an informational video for current and prospective church members. I video interviewed various leaders in the church about the services we provided, utilizing our new priest as the emcee for the video. My goal was to showcase the strong sense of community, service, and history that our small Catholic church provided. Not to mention, I hoped that it would act as a potential argument for keeping our Catholic school open, despite the decreasing attendance and financial support.

As I edited the video, I was once again reminded that faith was becoming a part of my journey. I remember completing the rough draft of the movie and showing my dad the ending clip. As we watched the final music begin to fade and the camera come to a halt at the cross above the church altar, I began to tear up. I was overwhelmed with the memories and milestones I had at that church.

I was overwhelmed as well at the history it told of our own family. My mom grew up and went to school in those walls. My mom walked down the aisle and said, "I do," to my dad. My own baptism, first communion, and confirmation occurred in those same spots. Despite my lack of attendance, Mallory had just gotten married there as well. So, I was overwhelmed with joy that this project had come together, and I recognized that it was exactly what I needed at that time to push forward.

Upon completion of the video, I submitted my project in its entirety. I turned the paperwork in before my eighteenth birthday, and I remember thinking, *Welcome to adulthood!* I had finally reached one of the goals I had set out to do in my last year of high school and I knew my mom would have been proud. She would have been with me through this milestone.

I didn't take part in an Eagle Scout ceremony until I was twenty-one, but I remember that moment as bittersweet. It was the feeling of reaching another level on my grief mountain while recognizing what I had to go through in order to get to that moment. Adding to that feeling, it was tradition in Boy Scouts that when a scout advanced in rank, the scout added a pin to his mother's ribbon. We had luckily found my mom's ribbon, embedded with all of the previous pins I had placed on as she proudly wore it. When I placed the last pin at the bottom, I laid it in front of a portrait of her that we displayed at the head table, a truly powerful moment.

I had started moving up my mountain again, but I wasn't done climbing. I continued the momentum in my last semester of school by focusing my energy on preparing for college. Through taking classes that would prepare me for the placement tests, applying for scholarships, and enrolling in an online music course, I was feeling as if I was coming back into a positive cycle of my life.

Even my college school of music audition brought a surprising amount of confidence back. I had researched and prepared the material I needed to audition with, and hit the road with my dad to show my future school what I could do. I may have been a little too confident for a collegiate audition by the way I dressed, though; I sported some blue jeans and a T-shirt. Looking back, I (and future classmates of mine who had seen my attire before the audition) was astounded at the fact I had been given a spot in the percussion studio. Maybe confidence truly is the key to anything. Or the phrase "Fake it till you make it" holds more weight than I'd thought. Either way, my future was looking up again.

"I'm so happy your audition went well. I knew you would make it in!" Jayme said, nudging me.

"Thank you. I don't know what I would be doing next year if I wasn't able to get into my own major right away," I said.

"You would have figured something out. You always do. Speaking of, have you figured out what you want to do for Valentine's Day?" she asked, winking.

I panicked. I had not been thinking about Valentine's Day—or our relationship for that matter, lately. I had been too focused on myself and all that I had in my head. Yes, I had been extremely selfish in that time, but I'd rather have given myself that self-care time than find myself in the aftermath of another anxiety breakdown. Learning to prioritize my self-care was a huge step forward from the many setbacks I had allowed myself.

I'm fairly certain that our Valentine's Day was typical—a dinner and a movie. My mind could be remembering that wrong, but what I do remember was feeling out of place. I was beginning to see Jayme as I had before we dated, which was as a trusted friend. The idea of being in a relationship with her, or anybody at that moment, was seeming lackluster. I was having the thoughts again that I may not have been ready to enter a relationship when I did.

Perhaps through my depressed cycle, I had come out with a clearer mind and was finally seeing through an unclouded lens. Through this clear lens, Jayme was the same sweet and genuine girl in our friend group with whom I enjoyed sharing my thoughts. I just couldn't force myself to put on the fake glasses again that made me see us as a couple anymore. She deserved to be listened to and treated the same way that she had done for me.

So, the day finally came when we both decided that our relationship needed to end. This was yet another bittersweet moment because I knew it was the right thing for us. Yet, at the same time, I knew how much she was probably hurting throughout those six months as I failed to truly be present for her. If it made her feel any better, I had failed to be there for my sister during her wedding, so I obviously had my issues to work out before I had a better hold of my grief.

Exiting that relationship did teach me a few things. First, I needed to always trust my gut. Peer pressure wasn't a good excuse to disregard my own mind telling me that I wasn't ready to fill any part of the void my mom left. Second, I was willing to wait for a relationship to come naturally. It was all right to have a different time line than my sisters—even if that meant I had to wait until I was in retirement to find someone! The main point was that I would wait until I was ready to open my heart fully.

With those realizations came inspiration for a long overdue song to be written:

In a couple of years, we'll see where God takes us.
We don't know where we'll go, but we know it's our road.
And honestly, you've let me be me.
So, there's no looking back; my mind is free

With you, I lose nothing
With you, I am something
With you, we sing[4]

Sydney and Jordan, *I can't wait for your first dance*, I thought as I finished their wedding song. I was getting excited for their big day.

My sister and her fiancée had set their wedding a week before my graduation. In a natural fashion, this time of year felt like a closing of a chapter. More importantly, this wedding was my redemption to show that my family was important to me and I wouldn't let anything get in the way of recognizing that. We were a family that would support each other in not only our worst times, but also in our milestones.

That support showed throughout her big day. I watched our extended family and friends fill the church and take on the various roles of the ceremony. I teared up as I saw my sister walk down the aisle with her dress that allowed her to show off the tattoo on her shoulder—a dedication to our mother.

The support came in whimsical ways as well.

"Lastly, our mom always wanted a redheaded child. She didn't get that, but I know she's going to be happy because she's going to have a redheaded grandchild," Mallory said as she finished her maid of honor speech. The whole reception hall burst out in laughter as we all gave a side glance to Sydney's new husband. He knew he had just entered a unique family dynamic.

To this day, I look up to my sisters and their husbands. Part of me is envious that they have found the person they want to spend the rest of their lives with and that my mom was able to meet both of them. Another part of me realizes that they, too, had to go through the process of putting their hearts out there and experiencing failure. They, too, had learned to get back up when they fell many times. They may have had mom to help them through those times, but they still experienced the bumpy ride.

Through the ups and downs of these intertwined rollercoasters of both grief and the world of love, I was learning to hang on. I didn't know when I was going to rise or fall; I may not have known or recognized which mood cycle I was in until it was too late, but I was beginning to enjoy the ride. The ride was easier if I pictured myself riding in the car with my mom as she purposely went over speed bumps, potholes, and race downhill just to give me "that feeling in your stomach, honey."

I guess she was teaching me from a young age to live on the edge and embrace the ups and downs of life. I had once again recognized I was in a positive cycle of my life. My hope was that I could rinse and repeat this cycle as I graduated and started my journey into college.

Perspective

THE DAUGHTERS (PART THREE)

Written by Sydney DeMaris

The hardest part about losing the best mom in the world is knowing my daughter will never get to know the best grandma in the world.

We went on with life. It wasn't easy at first, but we did it together as a family. The firsts without her were the toughest. I remember only about a week after her death having to go to my senior prom. This was supposed to be my last prom—the time of my life. All I wanted was for her to be there to help me get ready, do my hair, and experience another milestone in my high school career. Then, shortly after, was my graduation. I was supposed to be able to walk across the stage and go hug both my dad and my mom, hug the people who were my biggest supporters, but I only got to hug my dad. This was such a tough moment, emotionally.

My mom had such great friends, though, to help make those life events easier on my dad. The card club that my dad and mom were a part of made sure that we had the support. With helping out, to setting up and running my graduation party, we were not alone. Then it was moving to college. With each big event, I kept thinking, This is unfair! You are supposed to be here. Like I said, though, we *got through* those firsts and it especially helped when family was there.

It wasn't again until it was time to plan my wedding did it really start to hurt again. Wedding planning was supposed to be fun, but this wasn't fun at all. Knowing that she was supposed to be there to help me do it made anything I did just seem like work. This is when my mom started to come out in me—the inherited anxiety. I was nervous to go anywhere without the fear of feeling sick. It got to a point where I didn't even want to go out to church. It caused me to have multiple panic attacks, ultimately leading me to start taking anxiety medication. I truly felt like Mom then—seeing a little more into how my mom had felt with so much anxiety all those years.

I don't want to say that my wedding day wasn't the best because, after all, I married the man of my dreams. A man my mom knew. A man my mom trusted. I don't know if when she died she saw me marrying him, because we were only kids, but it's comforting knowing that they had met each other. My wedding day wasn't the "best" simply because she wasn't there. She wasn't there to hold my hand and get me through yet another life event.

Then again, we also didn't have Mom to hold our family together and make us be there for each other's special events. I've been regretting missing out on Sawyer's high school life. I know if Mom were there, she would have made Mallory and me go to more of his things. I would have hated it at the time but would be happy now. Yes, losing my mom close to my graduation was really hard for me, and I was going through so many big changes without her, but I still worried about Sawyer being so young and still at home. I should have stepped up and helped my dad with raising him—making sure he got decent meals like Mom would have cooked, doing the laundry, or cleaning the house.

Worrying about Sawyer became another thing that added to my anxiety. There was a time that he seemed sort of depressed and had texted me while I was at college. All the message said was, "I love you." Not that he couldn't say that, but it wasn't characteristic of him. I came home that weekend, worried that he had committed suicide. I panicked and the whole drive home that was all I could think about. Instead of going to Jordan's place, I went straight home. I went inside and searched every inch of our house, just scared I would find his dead body. I probably was just being irrational, and I probably never even tried to call him, but anxiety doesn't need to make sense to take control.

When the time came for Jordan and me to start trying to get pregnant, I knew I needed to take control over my anxiety so that I wasn't on the medication while I was pregnant. This is when I started dieting to feel better about my body—find a new way to cope and lose any weight gain that the medication caused. My biggest dream in life was to become a mother. I didn't want the anxiety and grief to take away that dream.

I don't know what was so appealing to me about being a mother or when that dream started. I know all girls grow up wishing for that, but I felt like I had this extra urge. Maybe I thought that it would fill some missing void, or just the fact that I really enjoyed kids. Maybe it was just the fact that I had the best mom ever. *Who wouldn't want to be just like her?* I told my husband before I married him that if he didn't want kids, I couldn't marry him. Well, when it was finally the right time in our lives, my husband and I started right away.

All throughout the whole process of trying to get pregnant, I sat at night, praying to my mom. "Please, Mom, bless me with a baby. Please let me be a great mom like you." Eventually, that blessing came in the form of my strawberry-blonde bundle of joy, Brynn Rebecca. My mom had made us kids promise if we ever had a redheaded baby, we would name it Lorelei—based off one of her favorite shows, *Gilmore Girls*. We came close with this mini-Becki Jo, but if I ever do have a true redheaded girl, I better honor my mom's wish!

I love being a mother just as much as I'd thought I would, and I love watching everything my daughter learns each day. Most of all, I love watching her little mannerisms that are exactly like my mother's. My mom had loved picking on me and teasing me—pinching me with her toes or putting her leg on me just to annoy me. This little girl does the same exact thing. She doesn't want to play with her toys; she just wants to pick on me, and I love every minute of it! Just like before I became pregnant, I still pray to Mom every night, asking her to watch over Brynn. I know she is answering my prayers.

I see my mom in the rest of my family as well. My dad has been the best dad/mom and has brought me through so much. He has been our constant and has always been there for us whenever and whatever we needed. More importantly, he was the best husband ever. He loved, and still loves, my mom so much. Even when my mom joked around that she was going to leave him for one of the Minnesota Twins players—Tori Hunter—he didn't care and just kept on loving her. She joked that my dad stalked her when they were younger and that she didn't like him. Nevertheless, he would still go to her place and sleep on her parents' couch. He was madly in love with her and stood by her side through everything—even sickness. Just the same, Jordan has been my rock and has dealt with my own crazy side. He was the one to silently lie with me on our living room floor the day that she died, and he has done the same through the years since then.

Mallory has been my mom and has helped me with any advice I would have asked my mom. Sawyer has been my inspiration in seeing how he is never scared to try new things; it has made me less scared to step outside of my own comfort zone. Brynn has been my "filler" to attempt to occupy the void my mom left. She has let me try to be the mom that my mom was, helping me to remember aspects of her. She has given me another person to love just as much.

My dad has been granted the same opportunity through Laurie. All my mom ever wanted for him was to find someone again. That's what all us kids ever wanted. Laurie was and is that person for Dad. At first, I thought Laurie was just helping my dad out with stuff, like the rest of the card club, taking him Christmas shopping or helping us around the house. I am so glad it became more, though. Laurie makes my dad happy again, and I am very thankful for that. I know that my dad has been cautious throughout it all to make sure it doesn't upset us kids. For me, though, it has been what has helped me because she was there for my dad when we couldn't be; she has been there for us kids during all of our milestones. I am happy my daughter gets to call her "Grandma," and I see how happy that makes my dad as well.

Throughout the years, things got easier. Soon, it wasn't anger and sadness when I thought of her. It was still, "I miss you," but more about remembering times and remembering the little things about her. I remember in college, whenever I missed my mom or had a really bad day, I called up my brother. No—not to talk to my brother—but to listen to my mom's voice on his voice mail. I wanted to hear her voice and imagine her giving me the advice that I needed. Her voice mail is gone, but I still can imagine what her voice sounds like. Now, I have a tattoo that serves as her voice—a butterfly on a gerbera daisy, with the words, "I Hope You Dance," inscribed on one of the daisy petals.

Yes, I want to be able to forget the bad times, but I also miss remembering the goodness those times have brought us too. I reflect back on mom's life and thank God that He made this amazing person that I needed to live more like. It worries me to this day that I am so much like her and that I may be the next one to get cancer, but that's the anxiety speaking. Was I better able to cope when I started to take care of myself? I don't know—but I was able to control my anxiety by myself without medications. The anxiety was still there, but it was manageable.

I hate to say that I have no grief now, but it has gotten smaller and has changed. I wish Mom was here, and I enjoy thinking about her, but I don't have that feeling of hurt when I miss her. Unfortunately, it's getting harder to remember her. I remember things about her, but I don't have her in my dreams much anymore or daydream about her. If I see something Brynn does that reminds me of her, or if I think about something we might have done with Mom, that's when I remember her. I don't know if I can be as strong as she was, but I try not to let things like that worry me and try to live my life like she did even after she was diagnosed. Brynn will never get to meet Grandma Becki, but she will get to know her—through me.

9 "I Hope You Dance"

The hardest part about finding comfort while grieving is allowing yourself to be vulnerable within new environments.

"And as we end our high school career, let us not forget that we will never again have to be part of a one-man devil pack. There are seventy-eight of us Green Devils graduating today, all united and ready to face whatever life brings us next. We won't let any obstacles get us down; but, instead, we'll turn it into something better. I guess that's why they call us the class of 2012!" I announced, finishing my speech from the graduation podium.

As the crowd gave their round of applause, I caught glimpses of the various friends and fellow graduates who had been united with me through what I had faced so far. In my speech, I'd applauded our class for its ability to remain resilient in the many uncomfortable situations we'd endured. Beyond my mom and Jana, we'd experienced the death of a beloved kindergarten teacher while we had been her students, the death of a music teacher who'd taught all of the Catholic school transfers, and we'd watched as many of our classmates' parents or family members had gone through their own cancer scares. Despite the many misfortunes that our small class withstood, we'd still made it to graduation because we'd somehow found comfort in each other.

Our minds are wired for comfort. We remember comfortable moments, places, people, events, and so on due to the feelings they evoke. In times of anxiety, comfort is what brings us back to reality, able to soothe the mind and soul. We enjoy comfortable moments because, for a joyous time, we can forget our thoughts or our pain and be focused on the present.

During my speech, my eyes were focused on the army of family who were there for my milestone: my dad, Laurie, my sisters and their husbands, all of my mom's sisters, my grandpa, and my grandma. I couldn't help but smile at the comfort I felt through their presence, and I relished this feeling; but I wondered when and how I would find this comfort again. How do I create comfort beyond these obvious milestones? The next chapter of my grief journey would be my quest to answer this question.

My graduation ceremony and reception that same day gave me a chance to bring closure to my previous chapter. That chapter was filled with many successes, but obviously held numerous somber moments that I can only hope made me a stronger person. We were celebrating the successes of my school years, but without words, we were honoring those who had led me to that point. That chapter ended fittingly with a graduation rose—a rose intended for the graduates' mothers but given to my grandmother in admiration and appreciation.

Finally, my next chapter had begun. I was moving to a bigger city two and half hours away from the comfortable small, Iowa town where I had experienced everything. I was trading up my own personal room for a small dorm room; trading the ability to drive with a reliance on the campus bus system and my own two feet; and trading up the comfort of knowing everyone I interacted with in order to meet complete strangers. Many things were about to change, but hadn't I already learned how to adapt and accept change? Change was going to be good.

The day I moved to my new city was exciting. After I set up my dorm room and settled in, I had to say goodbye to my dad, sister, and brother-in-law who'd helped move my stuff. Of course, I knew that I would be able to see them again and that they were only a phone call away, but symbolically, each child who moves on from graduation has this defining moment where they recognize his or her true independence. I had been ready for this moment. I had been prepared. I had repackaged my grief enough to be able to handle this independence.

My grief was now, very fittingly, the size of my laptop bag. I carried this bag with me whenever I could—to class, coffee shops, the music building, and back to my dorm room. The weight was much more manageable than my backpack because I knew that I couldn't allow too much to be shoved into my laptop bag, otherwise my walks around campus would take a bigger toll on me. I could recognize when it became too much. My lack of a car this first year of college represented me relearning how to get around within this new environment.

College, for me, meant a fresh start. I had a haunting set of questions that ruminated in my head a lot after graduation: What if my successes in high school were due to people feeling sorry for me? Was that why I was chosen for student leader positions or roles in school plays or musicals? Was that why I made friends easily—they were just being sympathetic?

I also wondered if teachers were giving me the benefit of the doubt the first couple of years after my mom passed away. To be honest, there were times I didn't attend my band or chorus lessons due to forgetfulness but still received full credit. Was there favoritism included in there? I liked to believe that it was due to my reliability and extra efforts outside of class that gave me this unfair perk, but the thought was still stuck in my head. This thought only became worse when a friend had admitted to me that he'd heard others say the same thing: "People just feel sorry for him. I think he uses his mom to his advantage." *Ouch.*

Whatever the reasons were, college would be a chance to prove those suspicions wrong. I was determined to be involved on campus, study hard, and aim for improvement in the talents I had. All of these new people that I would meet wouldn't know what I had gone through up until that point. I had the opportunity to live a different life and develop friendships that weren't based on sympathy. I would know for sure that the connections I made were based on who I was and not what I had been.

"Hey, I recognize you," someone said to me as I walked past her in the campus music building. I turned around and saw a familiar face. I instantly remembered her from the week after my school of music audition where we'd both attended the day-long honor-band event at the university. She was hard to forget because she was the first person I'd met who had a fairly unique and distinct talent.

"You were the girl that had perfect pitch, right?" I asked. I had a flashback to when she was able to tune the timpani without using the pitch pipe, as she explained that she had discovered in high school that she had the ability to distinguish pitches without help.

"Yep, I'm that girl," she said, looking down. I think I offended her by labeling her "that girl."

"Don't worry. I remember you well. Emily, correct? Not often do you meet another person who holds the title of two-time first alternate—Iowa All-State Band. We rejects have to stick together." I laughed. "What are you doing here?"

"I just got done with drumline auditions. I'm actually going to be in the percussion studio here," Emily explained.

"No way! I got into the percussion studio as well! I'm going to be studying music therapy. What about you?" I exclaimed.

"I'm interested in music education," she said.

"Well, I'm assuming we'll have similar classes," I declared, smiling. "I'm really glad that I at least know one person before classes start."

I left the music building that day amazed at how a simple encounter was able to ease my anxiety over starting college; I mean, this was only the first twenty-four-hours of moving. Clearly, I had a butterfly watching over me in this transition period. Maybe creating new friends would help me find the comfort I was looking for.

Thus, I was beginning to meet a plethora of new individuals. Like most universities, my first week experience involved many—dare I say, "too many"—new student orientations. At these orientations is where I met many new faces that I wouldn't talk to for the rest of my college career. Some of these people I had briefly run into at times during my first year, but the majority of my new friends seemed to be made in my music classes.

Just like high school, the connections I made revolved around music because I was able to express myself best through that medium. Emily and the other classmates in my percussion studio shared the same passion and similar interests. More importantly, I was assured that the interactions I had with these new friends and colleagues were not fake or done through sympathy. In fact, I had purposely avoided talking about my family or found ways to skirt around subjects that would lead me to explaining my grief.

"So, what do your parents do?" Paris, a music therapy classmate of mine, asked.

"My dad's a mechanic. What about siblings, do you have any?" I shot right back. I had rehearsed a similar situation like this in my head a couple of times. I didn't want to open up a can of worms too early.

I could tell that these new friends were curious as to why I didn't talk too much about my family life. I began to feel ashamed that I was once again keeping things to myself and not expressing my grief. However, I justified these actions by using the excuse, Well, I'm not totally keeping things in. I still talk to friends from high school. And, I'm not technically lying to anyone. I also thought that eventually I would tell them. Just not then.

This arrangement I made with myself seemed to be working. I was entirely positive that I wasn't being treated any different based on what I had experienced. Now, the worry was on the fact that at some point I had to be honest. Would that change my relationship with anyone? Would they begin to treat me in a different way or feel uncomfortable that I hadn't been honest with them? Similar to how I treated some of my homework and studying for classes, I decided to let those questions be answered at a different time.

I focused instead on being an active component of an organization that I knew I wanted to be a part of since high school—Dance Marathon.[1] When Mallory had attended the University of Iowa, I'd watched my sister get involved with this odd event where college students spent twenty-four hours dancing without sitting, sleeping, or drinking caffeine. In order to get to the event, they had to raise a minimum amount of money, which supported the local children's hospital. The event had always intrigued me due to its success of raising over a million dollars alone each year by students. Thanks to other hometown alumni, we had been able to set up an annual mini Dance Marathon event when I had been a freshman in high school. Through that event, I got a taste of what it was like to be an activist.

I knew I needed to be a member of this organization because their mission encompassed physical action against the same disease that took my mom and Jana. By joining the organization, I was committing to raise money year-round that would benefit children in the university hospital's pediatric oncology unit. I soon learned that 100 percent of these proceeds went to support these children financially and emotionally through pharmacy bills, restaurant gift cards, memorial stones for children who passed away, and various unexpected needs that arise when someone goes through treatment.

I began to feel the same empowerment that I'd felt when taking action throughout Jana's decline. I wasn't remaining passive in my continued search for how to cope with my grief. Fund-raising and attending meetings for this organization were active coping behaviors that I could use to feel like I was continuing to make steps forward; it helped me take back the power from the helplessness of life's losses. Unfortunately, when I tried to recruit some new friends to join with me, they didn't understand my obsession with being a part of the organization.

"Eh, I don't have time with drumline and classes. Sorry, I might try the event some other year," Emily said. "You can let me know how it goes!"

Another classmate decided not to hold back: "Those people are so annoying. They are constantly asking for donations and trying to recruit you wherever you go. Trust me: if you wanted to be in a cult, you're better off joining a fraternity. Speaking of, the music fraternity is looking for new members!"

I thought, Well, obviously my friends don't care about this issue as much as I do.

Yet it wasn't that my new friends didn't understand or care about the work Dance Marathon did—I was just overly anxious to take action. I wanted to work through my own grief by contributing to this organization because as other writers before me have found, active contributions can help us gain back power and confidence as well as help us prove that we still can make a difference.[2] I had seen firsthand how a high school classmate and friend of mine, Cally, had turned her mom's experience with breast cancer into an opportunity to start her own movement—Cally's Cause. Her movement supplies hand-quilted chemo bags filled with supplies for people to take with them as they receive treatment. I watched in admiration at Cally's efforts, recruiting our small community to grow the movement into a success that keeps growing. Now, each bag she sends to an individual with cancer provides that needed comfort in an otherwise unsettling environment.[3]

Not only do the chemo bags provide comfort for those in need, but our small-town community experienced similar satisfaction from being able to contribute to the cause. I noticed the same satisfaction and comfort during Jana's benefit and funeral, and I remember being surprised that I was able to recognize my own comfort despite the grief that was re-opening in that time. Feldman and Kravetz labeled this feeling, "grounded hope," in their book, *Supersurvivors*. Grounded hope refers to the belief that resilience is built, in part, through taking action. Through acting on realistic possibilities and goals, people can move forward from the permanence of a situation by shaping what is next.[4] Cancer may still be a disease, but we don't have to sit back and let it remain our problem. We can take back some control.

Therefore, as the first weekend of February rolled around, I was ready for my first experience of a true marathon of dancing. Thanks to friends and family donating in honor of my mom, I had fundraised enough money to participate in the Big Event. I was about to experience a day's worth of dancing, activities, and most importantly, hearing the passionate stories from many of the families that the organization supported. Each hour, a family of one of the children at the hospital had the spotlight on the stage to share their past and current journey through some of the roughest parts of their lives. They expressed how even the simple act of a Dance Marathon volunteer playing with their child in the hospital brought comfort to an otherwise exhausting and uncertain hospital stay. For families who had lost a child to cancer or leukemia, they expressed how the memorial stones given to them by Dance Marathon and the Dancing in Our Hearts memorial services brought them comfort in their grief.

In a moment that I will never forget, I heard the story that gave me an important perspective on grief:

"Our Gabe may have lost his battle a few years ago, but we cherished the time we had with him. We cherish the memories we made with him and love to share those stories. The hardest part about sharing this with people that we meet is noticing how people avoid the subject. They avoid using his name," Gabe's mother said.

"People avoid the subject because they don't want us to become upset. But when people avoid talking about our son, it feels like he never existed. We *want* to talk about him. We *want* to share stories of our unique little seven-year-old son that we were blessed to have. Talking about him honors his life and shows other people that we are doing all right," Gabe's father added.

In that moment, I looked up to this couple. They had spent less time with their son before losing him than I had with my mom. I had fourteen full years with my mom, and yet I was hesitant to share that she'd even existed with new people—let alone share personal stories like this couple was doing. I noticed the joy on their faces as they continued their story with a room full of eager listeners. Even though they had shared their grief, their message wasn't of sympathy, but a message of acceptance such as "this is our life" and "in order to know us, we want you to know our story." You need to confront the undeniable and treat grief like it were a physical impairment. Just like with a broken arm, this couple was showing their grief to others in order to address their obvious loss and in hopes that their audience might show their support by signing the metaphorical cast that helps to heal their grief.

The whole Dance Marathon experience put a lot of things into perspective. I had been approaching this new chapter in my life entirely wrong, possibly taking a step back in my quest to find the perfect formula for finding comfort within my grief. Therefore, shortly after that event, I decided to be honest with a few of my friends—Emily and Paris. These two had shared both their lives and musical talents with me, so I needed to reciprocate the former.

"I want to tell you two something. I've been avoiding this conversation for a while, but in order to truly know me, I want you to know about my mom," I began as the three of us sat in the dorm lounge. We had just finished performing together at a university talent show, riding a natural high. I shared only what I was able to in that moment, but even a small conversation was better than none.

I thank Gabe's family for the wisdom they shared so that I could realize how important it was to "keep the memory alive." Yes, waiting to tell new friends about my grief allowed me to make sure my relationships were not based on sympathy, but if I knew how much comfort I would receive from telling them my whole life, I would have told them sooner. This newly given wisdom came at the perfect time as another April 10 arrived and I found myself walking to class with an umbrella.

"Happy five years, Mom. Thanks for the storm."

* * *

As cliché as the saying goes, my first year of college "went by in the blink of an eye." In that year, I had proven to myself that I was willing to try new things. I had established a new comfort zone among my college friends and colleagues, which allowed me to feel empowered to take on new experiences. However, I credit most of this comfort from finding an active coping mechanism through Dance Marathon and my ability to acknowledge the importance of my mom's death in my own identity.

Similar to establishing music and faith as a part of my identity, I wanted to embrace my mom's death as my motivation to make a greater impact. As I'd told my fellow classmates in my graduation speech, we have already shown how to turn our obstacles into something better, so I was ready to work toward better. I remember looking at my list of college goals that I had written the summer before I started classes and I crossed each one of them out. What is a list of goals if they are easily attainable? I needed more challenging goals; goals that were not as self-absorbed. I started a list that would allow me to further expand my comfort zone, try new things, and use my talents in a positive action toward my grief and the grief of others.

One of the first goals centered around Dance Marathon. Yes, I had participated in the event already, but how could I get more involved? Was there a way I could raise more money or spend some more time helping families in the hospital?

"I'm making a CD," I suddenly declared. I had just finished a performance at an alumni event in my hometown. One of the facility staff, Cindy, had taken the time to ask me about my college career thus far and asked the usual, "What is next?" Not even I was expecting the answer I gave.

"Oh, of your own songs?" Cindy asked, intrigued.

"Yeah." I paused, thinking about that statement. "Yeah, I want to make a CD of my songs to raise funds for the children's hospital."

"Are you going to go to a studio for this?" she asked.

"No, my sisters bought me a microphone for Christmas a couple years ago. I've been messing around with it for a while and think I'm ready to make something like this happen," I said, getting more certain as I spoke.

"Wow, that's amazing! If I can help in any way, please let me know. If you want, I could even help with the CD design," Cindy offered. I remember knowing after my conversation with her that this interaction felt destined to happen. Just like that, something had been set in motion.

After exchanging information and leaving the venue, I had another gut feeling. Why did I just randomly share that idea with her? I had thought about a project like this before, but I'd never had the nerve to believe I would act on it, especially without proper resources. At the same time, this was just the project I needed to utilize my talents, open up my songwriting to a bigger audience, and increase my fund-raising without having to beg for donations.

The more I shared my CD project with other people, the more it became a reality. I had been writing songs since high school. At times, these songs were cryptic messages about my mom and how I was grieving; while, at times, they were simply proclamations of love that I am still embarrassed to read.

Nonetheless, I had enough songs with heartfelt messages—such as my sister's wedding song—that were perfect to make this CD possible. I began to wonder if my sisters knew what they were setting me up for when they bought me that first microphone.

After writing a song specific to Dance Marathon's message, I began recording the songs that I had chosen. In a makeshift studio from the bedroom I grew up in, I spent weeks making this project into what I had envisioned it to be—my retaliation effort against the disease that had taken my mom. As powerful as their stories were to hear, I dreamed of a day that the families of the children at the hospital wouldn't have to grieve over their sons or daughters dying so young. No, my CD wouldn't prevent someone from dying, but the money raised could provide the emotional support needed to lessen the grieving process.

Within a couple of months, I had completed my CD. Holding a physical copy in my hand proved that it was real. I was just thankful that my hometown community was willing to help in many ways throughout the process, providing a free photoshoot, CD design, a press release, and venues to sell copies. Once again, it was proven that I needed to trust myself when I had a gut feeling.

The day of the CD release proved to be equally as humbling. The restaurant I worked at allowed me to hold a "give-back" day for Dance Marathon and an open mic night to promote the CD. After performing one of the original songs from the album, I ran into Laura, a waitress who had been walking around the crowd of people, selling the CDs.

"I think you'll want to take a look at this," Laura said, handing me a stack of money. All I could see were numerous one-hundred-dollar bills. "Some guy just bought one CD and gave me this."

"Laura, there's $500 here! Is he drunk? Does he need change?" I asked, laughing.

"No, he told me to keep it all," she said and added, "He said he is one of Jana's cousins. He recognized you from her funeral."

In that moment, I comprehended how powerful of a notion the CD had already become. The process of making the CD was therapeutic for me, but the product was certainly being acknowledged as a memorial for others. Each donation meant further support. There was also a validation at that time that I needed to continue to pursue music therapy as a life path. Music was giving me a voice of action.

As my second year of college started, I had already surpassed enough donations to attend the next Dance Marathon Big Event. Regardless, I was insistent on continuing my efforts, especially as I started my leadership journey for Dance Marathon that year. As loosely correlated as it was at times, I attributed my involvement in any event for this organization to be a connection with my mom. I felt that if she were still alive, she would be supporting me in my endeavors.

This connection was made clear to me once I met the Mumme family. The Mummes were one of our Dance Marathon families whose son, Dillyn, had battled leukemia throughout his high school career. Having just completed his last chemo treatment the previous year, Dillyn was entering college at another university with the proud accolade "Survivor in Remission." I recall my first encounter with him at my first Dance Marathon event where he captivated the crowd with his heartfelt story of going through treatment. I was certain after his speech that I wanted to someday be as vulnerable as him in sharing my grief. For now, I was taking those smaller steps of vulnerability by establishing my comfort level.

Through stroke of luck, or divine intervention, my position in leadership was partnered with the Mumme family, allowing me to express my admiration.

"You are an inspiration, Dillyn. I still wonder how you went through all of those procedures and remained so strong. Not to mention, how you were able to speak so freely about your experiences" I said at our first meet-up at a family event for the organization.

Being as humble as he is, Dillyn downplayed it. "I was just speaking from the heart."

"What about you? I saw the song you wrote for Dance Marathon. I even shared it on Facebook," Dillyn's mother, Tammy, chimed in. "That's a unique idea to sell CDs to fund-raise."

It was then my turn to be humble as we began discussing the unexpected impact of the CD thus far.

Within our conversation that day, I did something uncharacteristic of myself up until that point—I didn't hesitate to open up. After hearing Dillyn's story again, I wanted to be honest from the start when the Mummes asked me about my own family. These were new people to me, but yet, I felt comfortable sharing the simple fact that I lost my mom to cancer. This family had gone through their own grief through Dillyn's treatment; I knew they would understand.

"I knew there was something about you ever since I heard your song," Tammy added.

That day started a unique relationship with what we jokingly call "my other family." I began to share personal milestones with them as they kept me involved in Dillyn's journey to hit the five-year cancer-free mark. This relationship came at a perfect time.

After my phone buzzed for the third time in a row, I thought, Why do I keep getting calls from Dad? At the time, I was interviewing potential leaders for the university's week-long orientation program that I had been helping with. The second that one of the interview rounds had concluded, I stepped out into the hallway to make a call.

"You called?" I asked, as my dad answered the phone.

"I was just trying to reach you to let you know something," he replied. I had an uneasy feeling that I knew what this phone call was about. He continued, "I went into the hospital the other day to finally get a checkup. Mal and Syd have been pushing me to do this for years." He hesitated. "I thought you should know that the doctors found cancer on my back. It's melanoma, skin cancer."

For a second, I had a flashback to the same moment my mom told me a similar sentence—that moment where my mom hugged us children and she cried over the uncertainty. Yet, within another second, I lost the uneasy feeling. I heard the phrase "Don't worry" in my head as I calmly replied to my dad, "What happens next?"

"They will want to do surgery to remove it from my back. They also need to do some tests to see if it has spread anywhere," he explained. "I will keep you posted."

Despite hearing that news, I still was sure that the situation again presented before our family wasn't the same as my mom. I felt calm and entirely positive that the uncertainty would pass. Was this my young naïveté again? Or was it blind optimism? No. Was I just blocking out the negative emotions again? No. I had learned too much about my own grief to know avoidance wasn't healthy. I was simply experiencing feelings of comfort through yet another gut feeling.

Despite my comfortableness, I shared the latest news with the Mummes and continually kept them informed. After I received the text from Laurie letting all of my dad's family know his surgery was a success, I relayed that news to the Mummes. After the doctors conducted a dye-test to see where the cancer could have spread, my dad went through an additional surgery to remove a lymph node as a safety precaution. I was then able to let the Mummes know the news that my dad was declared cancer-free within a short, but eventful, month! To this day, Tammy or Dillyn will typically start our interactions off with, "How is your dad?" And to this day, I am able to continue to say he is cancer-free.

Through both my dad's cancer scare and my ability to confide in the Mummes, I realized that there were ways for me to find comfort in my grief journey. I didn't mean the comfort experienced through everyday things that I enjoyed doing, or the comfort of sleeping in a warm bed, or even the comfort of hitting natural milestones like my graduation; I meant the comforting feeling I used to have with my mom around. I was recognizing that these moments, the moments where I was vulnerable with new friends, had allowed me to experience the real comfort I was looking for all along.

Thus, as the week of my second Dance Marathon Big Event came, I chose to confide my full story for the first time with some fellow leadership members. I was running off a natural high of the success of my CD bringing in over $3,000 in donations for that year, and the excitement of the big day approaching. My friends David and Erin sat with me in an empty Taco Bell as I shared with them my personal story and reason for dancing for the organization. I could see in their faces that they fully understood why I had become so passionate in Dance Marathon's mission.

I felt liberated as we left the fast-food joint out into the snowy, February night. As we walked up to our cars, I heard Erin's voice.

"Oh, weird, what is that?" she asked, pointing at my car's hood.

"Looks like a snow face," David added. I walked closer to see what they were admiring, and I saw the image dead center on my car.

"No." I laughed. "That's a butterfly." I was smiling in disbelief. My car's hood had been completely bare before I'd walked into the restaurant, but through the light snowfall, a beautiful image had fallen into place.

In my head, I heard an apt phrase being sung in my mom's comforting voice:

"And when you get the choice to sit it out or dance, I hope you dance."[5]

10 "Edelweiss"

The hardest part about vocalizing your grief is exposing your vulnerability for all to see.

Bookstores have always captured my heart. Walking into the smell of freshly pressed pages and a hint of coffee from the café in the corner. Aimlessly wandering around for books that you didn't even know you needed. Admiring books that you have already read and feeling the pressure to buy the commemorative set despite owning each individual book in the series. What a sight to see!

"Why do you want to go to the bookstore again? You didn't want to buy any new books the last couple of times we went, and when I do buy you a book, it sits on your book shelf," my mom asked.

"Why do I have to go to the mall with you, Mal, and Syd? You spend hours trying on clothes that you're not going to buy and buying clothes you're not going to wear," I responded. My mom had a hard time getting angry when I threw logic, or as she called it, "sass," back at her because she knew I got that trait from her. She would just give me a smile that communicated, touché.

The simple answer to my mom's question was that bookstores brought me into my comfort zone. I enjoyed reading the words of various authors and the stories they were able to unravel within the book's pages. Just like a flower taking its time to bloom, a story's depth and beauty show when it finally opens up—a beauty displayed for others to see its vulnerability.

Fictional stories had always been my preference for their ability to spark my own creativity. Fictional stories were an easy way to get away from reality and focus on an imaginary character's struggles over imaginary situations in an imaginary universe.

However, as I was beginning to vocalize my own story, I developed an admiration for the nonfictional world of books. How were these authors freely able to put their own struggles into words so eloquently? How were they so comfortably able to vocalize the wisdom they had learned in their darkest times? I wondered if they had ever suppressed their stories as I had during my early college years or had anxiety over telling simple facts about their stories to new people. I think of classics, such as C. S. Lewis's raw telling of his own grief journal, *A Grief Observed.*[1] That was unedited vulnerability at its finest.

Still, I've yet to walk into a bookstore and find that perfect self-help book, titled *Vocalizing Grief: Finding Your Vulnerability.* Vocalizing your own grief is a process that develops on its own time line and differs from person to person. There is no definitive ten-step process to grief coping that works for everyone. I've met people who are able to be open about their emotions from the moment they experience a loss or trial in their life. Dillyn was a clear example of this type of professional storyteller. I've also met people, specifically some of my clients, who believe that they are not allowed to express their own grief in front of other people so as to not "sound depressing." Their belief is that their story is not worth telling.

I've always personally struggled with telling my own story and showing what was truly going on in my head. I wanted to put off a persona that "had it together." I wanted to be the person supporting others and helping them through their own baggage. I wasn't humble enough to admit that even I needed to seek counsel in others—at least until I experienced that first anxiety attack in high school. I was brought back down to earth from the alternate reality I was living in, a magical reality where I didn't need support. I was then able to start the ascent up the steps to vulnerability. After I received the greatest butterfly from my mom on the hood of my car, though, I saw it as a sign that I had found my own steps to vocalizing grief—or better yet, exposing grief.

I initially viewed the snow butterfly as a stamp of approval for the route I had taken in college, especially coming at the specific time that it did. But the moment I saw the butterfly on the hood of my car, I thought I was reading one of those fiction books I used to get lost in; yet this wasn't fiction. My life had now become a Lifetime movie, and my story was worth sharing!

Just weeks after the snow butterfly incident, I received the news that I would be getting the opportunity to share my story with a broader audience.

"Guess who just made Catholic HEART Workcamp staff!" I instantly texted my high school youth minister, Beth, after taking a screenshot of the website announcement. I had been refreshing the website page every two seconds that day for the mission-trip company that I had attended for the previous five summers.

I had always dreamed about being on the mission-trip

staff after my first trip as a camper. That first mission trip had been only a year after my mom had died, and at that time in my life, I hadn't been able to be too far from a piano without feeling stressed. I'd found an old piano in the school that we had been staying at that week and had gotten my piano fix in each day. By chance, the staff musician, PJ, had walked by and decided to sit and listen. We hadn't verbally talked about my mom, but PJ had listened to me play the songs on my mind as well as one of my first original songs. In a nonverbal way, he had been one of the first new faces that I had been vulnerable with after my mom had died. Nevertheless, through a verbal conversation with my dad, who had been acting as one of the male chaperones for our parish that trip, PJ had learned why I had been clinging to music.

That week experience, along with the following four years' mission trips, had been active components in my turning to faith. I had found the comfort from my anxiety and felt closer to my mom during those trips without realizing the real reason why. I'd thought I had been enjoying the trips due to the meaningful work, energetic staff, nightly programs of funny skits and music, and the fact that I was finally traveling the States; but it had been moments such as the one I'd had with PJ that had kept me coming back. My growing faith had been giving me meaning and comfort so I could one day develop a voice to expose my grief to a bigger audience. Inside the CD I'd bought from PJ, he had commented on my story and my music, simply stating, "Share it with the world."

Five years after that first mission trip, I was finally getting my opportunity to share my story. I was going to be a staff member who could hopefully be an inspiration to teens and young adults just as the staff had been for me. My Lifetime story could possibly relate to someone else and bring the necessary words that might bring comfort to a grieving heart. *No pressure.*

Catholic HEART placed me on a team of nine individuals, including myself, that would be traveling the western United States. After completing our training in the company's home office in Orlando, Florida, my team set out on a seven-week-long summer tour to set up, run, and help manage six mission-trip camps in six different western cities. Our first camp required us to drive from Orlando to Reno, Nevada, with our truck, cargo van, and minivan packed full of our supplies and personnel. This first week of traveling allowed me to get to know my team better as we were about to spend a whole summer together.

The traveling time also allowed me to formulate the witness talk I was going to be giving during each week's Wednesday night program. This specific witness talk was coined the "story of healing" due to its placement before the Wednesday night tradition of "Four Corners," which was a time for campers to either pray alone, with each other, with an adult or staff member, or attend reconciliation with a priest, or all of these. Seeing as I am not known to be short and concise with my words, it was a blessing and a curse for my "story of healing" to be allotted only seven minutes. If I found myself having a hard time speaking each week, at least I only had to survive seven minutes in the spotlight.

When our first Wednesday arrived, I felt anxious. I was both excited to be taking this important step for myself by being vulnerable and also nervous about honoring my mom in a way that wasn't going to be using her memory selfishly. I didn't want people feeling *sorry* for me. I simply wanted to showcase how important it was to express your emotions and find solace in your own faith—especially for these teenagers and young adults who were going through their own journey to find and express themselves in an ever-changing teenage world.

"What is your talk about?" Erica, one of my teammates, asked.

"Can we get a sneak preview?" added Monica, another teammate.

At the time, we were all in the kitchen of the school we were working at and preparing that night's meal while the campers were still at their worksites in the community. I looked at both of them nervously and decided that it was probably best if I give a synopsis of my story to some of my teammates before coming out of nowhere with my plot twist.

I began recollecting the story I perfectly crafted the previous night, using this opportunity as my practice for the bigger audience that night. As I shared the death of my mom, the butterflies I received, and the most recent story of the butterfly on the hood of my car, the three of us embraced in a hug that eased my nerves about speaking. At the same time, another teammate of ours, Danielle, walked into the kitchen with something in her hand.

"Hey, Erica, here are the rags that you wanted Nate and me to get at the store," she said, showing us some colorful rags with familiar images on them. The three of us disengaged from our hug and looked at each other with tears in our eyes.

"What happened?" Danielle asked, puzzled.

"Out of all things, did you really have to bring us rags with butterflies on them!" Erica said, laugh-crying. Danielle was even more puzzled before we filled her in on the chapter she missed.

As I stepped on stage that night to finally give that first speech, I took a deep breath and reminded myself, "Someone in the crowd needs to hear this right now. Help them find the comfort that you have found." My team had just prayed over me backstage, showing their support in the step I was about to take. As I was beginning to speak in the microphone, they took their seat off to the side to be witness to my premiere showing.

"Hi, everyone. As you know, my name is Sawyer, and I've the honor of leading us into our Four Corners experience tonight. The story I'm about to tell encompasses a lot of my faith, but it revolves around two things: music and butterflies."

Those seven minutes became another turning point for my grief—a more innocent take on "seven minutes in heaven." I recalled my journey thus far and got choked up as I had to reveal the unhappily ever after that my mom's death day brought. I was verbally reliving that day's memory for the first time, watching the audience's reaction as I continued the true-life tale. I ended my story of healing with the image of the snow butterfly, and I will never forget the gasp I heard from the crowd. My breath was taken away as well as I stared up at the image projected for all to see on our screen.

I walked off the stage, and tears instantly started pouring. Within seconds, my team had rushed to my side, and I was scrunched in a hugging pile. These were a mixture of tears of joy and tears of sadness, knowing that my mom would have been leading the hugging pile if she had been with me. Nevertheless, I found myself pulling it back together in time to join the Four Corners experience and sit with various campers who wanted to talk or pray with me. After my willingness to be vulnerable, these teenagers took the example and professed some of their struggles with me, struggles ranging from typical school drama to serious suicidal ideation that prompted cautionary action with the camper's youth minister and parents. I was seeing the impact that exposing my own grief could make. It truly set an example.

I continued this routine of speaking and listening to campers each week that summer. I found that vocalizing my grief became easier as the weeks went by, helping to ease the residual pain and bringing light to the statement: "Grief shared is grief abated."[2] Vocalizing my grief also became easier due to the similar stories campers and chaperones were sharing with me each week, putting into perspective the different forms of mental and emotional pain that other teens and young adults experience.

"I remember my grandma whenever I see a penny," one camper said.

"Blue jays are my dad's symbol."

"I just lost my mom to cancer this year, and I really needed to hear that. Thank you," an adult chaperone said.

"Sawyer! We saw two butterflies at our worksite today, and the resident we were helping gave us this jar after we told her your story," a camper said, showing me a mason jar with a plastic butterfly that flew around when you pushed a button.

I continued to hear more and more people tell me that they were seeing numerous butterflies each day, despite the fact that summer was peak butterfly season. I couldn't help but laugh and think, I didn't mean every butterfly was a sign—just the unexpected ones. I was missing the point, though. If people were finding positivity and faith through every butterfly after hearing my story, why bother correcting them?

Even after ending tour that year, I was looking for more ways to tell my story in venues such as the mission trips. I was lucky enough to have one of the parishes that attended one of the mission trips reach out to me to speak at their school assembly that winter. The school was only a half-hour drive from University of Iowa, and their assembly was in preparation for their own mini Dance Marathon event. They asked if I would share my story along with the importance of Dance Marathon donations. *Perfect!*

I knew that as I was preparing to talk with this school,

there would be some students who had already heard my story. At the same time, there were students and teachers who would be hearing it for the first time as well. The realization dawned on me: If people are hearing this story for the first time, doesn't that mean they are processing my grief for the first time as well? Even if they weren't experiencing the grief firsthand, they would be subjected to the emotions of grief that I had been able to process over many years. They were hearing it for the first time.

Unfortunately, in all my stages of learning how to vocalize my grief and tell new people about my mom's death, I had forgot that my listeners needed the time to process the plot twists as I did. Granted, they never knew my mom; but they were getting to know me. They were forced to accept the unchangeable truth as I had to when Jana had first said the words, "She gained her angel wings this morning."

Had I become insensitive to others by compacting years' worth of processing into seven minutes? I couldn't answer that, but I knew that I needed to use this school speaking engagement to slow down and recognize that others needed more time to sort out the anticipatory grief, initial shock, understand the multilayered grief and how I began to repackage and peel away its layers, and see how I was finding meaning and comfort through my mom's symbol of hope.

Fortunately, I found myself able to slow down and let the story unfold naturally as I spoke. I was beginning to find a new avenue of expression for myself with this faith and motivation speaking because I was able to unpack more of my grief and declutter my thoughts.

The same couldn't be said for my college schedule that year as I packed in the most semester hours that I could, started a new part-time job, accepted the position of event director for Dance Marathon, and continued my other extracurricular activities. By the time my junior year of college was over,

I was relieved my schedule could finally slow down again. That's when I found myself at the whim of my second (and hopefully last) anxiety attack.

* * *

"Cue the reality detachment. Bring in some more sweat. No! Even more! And where's Fear? He was supposed to make his entrance along with Crazy."

My mind was taking control of the story again. It was bringing me back to my high school musical and directing itself in a direction that I thought I steered clear of before. Combined with a physical fever I was recuperating from, this anxiety attack was an unwanted end-of-finals celebration gift. Why am I here again? The attack felt unprompted and, at the same time, prompted. The last time I'd had an anxiety attack, I'd recognized that it was due to me keeping my grief bottled up. This time, I wasn't quite sure if it had anything to do with my grief or if it was my body's reminder that self-care can't be ignored.

Either way, I came out of my anxiety attack, and the thoughts started rushing through my head. I began thinking about all of the friends from high school I hadn't talked to in a while. The same ones who'd brought me out of my anxiety the first time. Cortney. Drew. I even pulled out my phone, looking at the last time I had contacted them—their annual birthday texts. For some reason, I just couldn't type up a new message and hit send. I didn't want to bother them after all this time. Instead, I let a growing gut feeling fester inside.

I found a way to pull it together for the start of my second Catholic HEART tour that next week. I needed this new adventure to get me out of this odd cycle that I'd dipped back into. A new team. A longer allotted time for my witness talk. A shorter tour. And new locations. *This is what I need.*

It didn't take me long to turn a new page and continue writing and telling my story. Despite this continued gut feeling, I found comfort in my new team. They further brought out the growing Christian in me. Nostalgia hit me hard when I was able to reunite with PJ again for the first time in six years—this time, working with him, and this time, he was hearing me verbally vocalize my grief. My, how far I've come in those six years, I thought. I was picking up more confidence in myself each week as I spoke on stage. I grew more attached to my faith, especially as I presented a skit with my fellow teammates each week.

Within the skit, my character quoted a famous Bible verse, Philippians 4:13 (NLT): "For I can do everything through Christ, who gives me strength."[3]

Though that line was intended for laughter from its placement in our skit, I liked to believe that I was meant to be the one to say that line all along. By divine intervention, I was intended to hear and speak that phrase as a reminder; the further proof being in my character's name. Drew—the same name that was a tangible strength for me in my early grief journey. Cue more of that gut feeling.

My tour was shorter that year due to my need to be back at college to fulfill some summer duties of the event director role for Dance Marathon. I was distraught to end this humbling experience too soon, but I was also ecstatic for what was next. We were headed to the national Dance Marathon Leadership Conference in Baton Rouge, Louisiana, the climax to this gut feeling.

"Sawyer, have you heard anything from back home?" asked Katie, an old high school classmate and Dance Marathon delegate from a neighboring college. We were both waiting for the keynote speaker in the main auditorium at the conference.

"No, what do you mean?" I asked.

A pause. "I need to be the one to tell you. Before you start getting texts," she said as she handed me her phone.

My heart was pounding. I hadn't felt anticipatory grief quite as strong as this before. I was scrolling through her phone, reading text exchanges from Katie and her sister, Jayme. Yes—that Jayme. As I scrolled, my gut feeling was confirmed, and a tragedy *had* occurred: Drew had died.

I looked up at Katie, confused. I had so many questions, as did she. All I knew was that it was an unexpected death, a freak accident while on deployment with the air force. I didn't have long to talk to Katie before my fellow Dance Marathon delegates piled into the auditorium where I was now sitting with my hand covering my mouth. The lights dimmed, and our keynote speaker began his presentation.

I wasn't able to focus on the speaker, despite how important he felt his message was. My mind grappled with another layer of grief, a new form of unexpected grief. My grandpa's death had been unexpected, but he *was* getting old, and I never really got to know him well. And I at least had some fair warning with my mom and Jana's death as they spent their years in treatment. The only warning I got in this case was Katie breaking the news to me before—as she guessed it—I'd received texts one after the other. Cortney. My dad. Missed phone calls: three.

In what felt like forever, the keynote finally finished, and we were filing out of the auditorium, my face emotionless and my head and heart numb. I was simply following my colleagues' leads until we stopped to regroup in the lobby.

Tracey, our school's Dance Marathon adviser, took a look at me, and her smile went away as she asked, "Are you okay?"

I burst into tears, and she simultaneously whisked me away to a private area before any of my colleagues could say a word. She remained calm as she simply asked, "What's wrong?" *Everything*. I remained silent for a brief moment.

I think what she was really trying to say was, "Can you be vulnerable with me?" To that, I did know the answer. Time to expose my grief.

Tracey listened to me share memories I had of Drew. She was emulating what Drew had done for me with my mom. She comforted me enough so that I could take a breather and actively process my grief instead of suppressing it. She simply asked about this man she never knew, intrigued at every memory she somehow got me to apprise. In that moment, she was both the mom and friend that I no longer had. I was calm enough to head back to my room and work through my thoughts.

This grief was different. It hit me in a different way. Yet, I still had the tools to sort through the emotions—the most pressing of which was frustration toward God. How could He allow this to happen to someone so young? I had thought my faith was helping me through my grief. Now, my faith was further causing it? What about his family? His brother was at basic training for the air force. I thought, How would this affect him? I can only imagine what that family is going through.

I wanted to remain mad at God, but I thought back to my anxiety attack. I originally thought it had been unprompted, but what if it was just foreshadowing this unexpected chapter in my story? The anxiety attack prompted me to think of Drew and I almost reached out to him because of it. If only I did. What about my character's name and message in the skit? That's too much of a coincidence to say that God wasn't using my summer tour to prepare and strengthen me. He prepared me to expose my grief as soon as I could, and I wanted to believe that he was also preparing me to take it a step further through positive action.

When my mom died, I noticed the overabundance of people asking me, "Is there anything I can do?" or "How can I help?" Through my initial grief, I was too numb and shocked to know the answer to those questions. I wanted my mom back, but no one could help me with that. The questions became another annoying phrase to add to my list because I was too flustered to answer. Those people meant to be supportive, but I found more support from the people who did something such as bringing my family baked goods, teachers extending my homework deadlines, and friends making lip-synch videos with me hours after her death. I wanted to be one of those people who *did* something. My mom's voice was faintly heard again in my head, singing, "When you get the choice to sit it out or dance ..."

Dance. I sent out a distress call to old high school friends and started the conversation. We made plans to meet up as soon as I could get back from my conference and back to my hometown. I wanted to use the tool that brought all of us together with Drew, creating a lasting memory that would allow us to actively grieve together and physically show our support for his family. We were recording a CD.

"Drew was the common denominator for all of us in this room. Some of us probably have not even spoken since high school, but we are all here because we are grieving over a friend. These songs we are recording today are the songs we used to sing with him in this very room. All of those early mornings and late-night rehearsals for show choir, musicals, contests—you name it—were made even more special with his presence. He was here with us, being that comedic and supportive relief that we needed each day. Singing without him will be hard, but I promise you, letting the music start the conversation will help you vocalize this grief," I announced to a room full of tearful individuals who it gave me comfort to see again.

The memory of live recording this impromptu CD is another one that will forever be etched in my emotional memory. We took ourselves on a musical journey back through the years of high school by singing our men's ensemble classics, such as "Come Go with Me"[4] and "Fergus an' Molly."[5] We ended the CD, aptly titled *Drew's Legacy,* with the traditional Irish blessing[6] sung at every spring concert in our high school choir years. Chills ran down my spine as we all began singing the first line: "May the road rise to meet you." Vulnerability at its finest.

The last touch I wanted to add to the CD was a suggestion from my choir teacher. Drew had starred as Captain von Trapp in the school's rendition of *The Sound of Music*. The last song on the CD was going to be the audio of Drew singing "Edelweiss."[7] As the Drew's Legacy Choir, we would be getting the chance to sing that song at his funeral, but for the CD, Drew deserved his solo. His voice also needed to be heard. His voice would expose all of our grief in ways we could not. Thus, as we presented his CD to his family, I realized we had given them an abiding gift that they didn't know they needed. Our choir skipped the "How-can-I-help?" question and went straight for an answer: a Becki-approved answer shown by the kaleidoscope of butterflies flying outside of Drew's house as I dropped off the CD to his family.

I wish I could say that this funeral was easier than the numerous I had already had to be a part of. I wish I could say that experiencing new grief and loss as you got older would be more manageable after you've had a couple losses under your belt, but that's not the truth either. I also wish that I could write that less tears were shed at this funeral, but I would again be lying. Grief hits hard each time and tries to change up how it deals the blow to keep you on your toes. That shouldn't stop you from exposing it for its weakness. Grief cowers in the presence of family and friends' support. It doesn't know how to respond when you embrace your own vulnerability and vocalize your sentiment. Think about it—even a nasty rumor dies faster and is less enjoyable once the subject of the rumor plays along.

As I sat at the piano during his funeral, looking out at the congregation as I had done in similar times, I couldn't help but notice more of the faith I relied on. I wouldn't have been able to attend the funeral if I had done a full summer tour with Catholic HEART. I would have been miles away from the home and the support, arriving the day after his memorial took place. Additionally, the chance to expose my grief through music would have been missed. I wouldn't have been able to give one last thank you to a friend who helped me stay strong through other funerals. Note to self: never accept that God and my faith have abandoned me.

"Today's reading was picked by the family as the same verse tattooed on Drew's arm," the pastor began.

I thought, Wait, when did Drew get a tattoo?

"Philippians 4:13 states ..." the pastor continued.

Oh, now you're just playing with me, God.

Again, there is no foolproof process to learning how to vocalize your grief. Every loss is a new, definitive chapter. For some people, that's the beginning of their book; for others, that loss is simply a continuation of a long-standing plot. My plot had me spending my journey thus far using music to nonverbally grieve, taking those baby steps to feeling comfortable enough in new settings to verbally expose my emotions and expose the grief. Music slowly opened me up to lasting friendships and songwriting, which eventually helped take my words off page. When the time came, I knew I wanted to guide others in finding that strength sooner.

Therefore, had I now repackaged my grief from my laptop bag into a new container—a book? Not quite. Need we remember that if we continue to view our grief journeys as chapter books, we may be disheartened to know that the book is ever-growing, and we already know the ending includes loss. Drew's funeral gave me my new container—the edelweiss. For even in the harshest of winters, this small and bright flower blooms on the highest of mountains; exposing its essence for all to see.

Perspective:

THE NIECE/GODDAUGHTER

Written by Meghan Helmueller

The hardest part about losing a godmother is no longer sharing a tiny portion of an already packed sofa at a family get together; laughing and snuggling as her presence alone takes away my anxiety.

Becki was the "cool" aunt. She was also my godparent. This meant that she had an excuse to spoil me whenever she wanted to. I always looked forward to visiting her and to seeing what prank she would pull on our family. On a few occasions, I even stayed a week with her and her family during the summers. But she went beyond being an aunt and godparent—she treated me like her own daughter, which made her death even harder to deal with.

Toward the weeks leading up to Becki's passing, I prayed for her every night. Not to heal her; but to give her peace and strength. I knew her time was near when we had a family gathering at my grandparents' home and I saw Becki's physical appearance. She had lost several pounds and was very tired and weak.

One memory I still hold dear was of Mallory and Becki lying on the floor of the spare bedroom in their house, talking about meeting her maker. She seemed no longer fearful of dying; she was mostly sad for her children and husband who she would be leaving behind. I apologized for barging in on their conversation but yearned for time with Becki. She cleared a small spot next to her, and I laid down. She knew I was going through a tough breakup with my daughter Ella's dad. She said, "You know you are very special, and you should not settle. Don't be unhappy in your relationship. Life is too short." I've always remembered those exact words and have shared them with several people in times of separation.

With her ten-year anniversary coming soon, I have a lot of unanswered questions that I've been wanting to know over the years. Living in Wisconsin and away from Becki's family in Iowa made it harder for me to know what was going on. I remember my mom telling me that Becki had died and that her kids and Bruce were all there when she was at the hospital. She had also said it happened fairly quickly and that none of the extended family could have made it there in time. Becki wouldn't have wanted it to be a big show anyways. I just couldn't imagine what they were going through. Many times, my thoughts were with them, and we were asking the same questions: What were Becki's last words to Bruce and the kids? How are Mallory and Sydney doing at college? What was it like for them to plan weddings without their mother? How is Sawyer getting through high school without a mom? How can Bruce be so strong through all of this?

Personally, I've experienced a few losses in my own life. One of those losses being when my mom and dad divorced when I was in high school. I've supported my mom, Terri, in her relationship after her divorce and watched her heart get broken again. But I still can't imagine what the heartbreak has been like for her—having lost two siblings once Becki died. We don't seem to talk about it much, especially as the years have passed. It became even harder when we were making fewer trips to Iowa to see the rest of the family. God knows how long it has been since we've had our gigantic extended family Christmas festivities at our grandparents' house.

Then my brother got married in August of 2016. The wedding was the first wedding in my immediate family and was held on my mom's farm. The day was beautiful—with kids, grandchildren, extended family, and even chickens running around. What made the day more special was the fact that most of our extended family were able to attend. It felt like a mini family reunion, and one that we desperately needed. We finally had a day where we all could be celebrating together instead of attending another funeral.

But that day brought back so many emotions. A mixture of my mom's recent loss of a boyfriend of many years, anxiety over my own daughter's health and well-being, and seeing Bruce, Sawyer, and Sydney again brought me to tears that night.

"I need a Becki hug," I said to Bruce and Sawyer in the chicken shed.

They both embraced me as I cried. I had so much bottled-up emotions, and I needed Becki's embrace. A simple Becki hug would have been enough. I didn't have that option anymore, so I found myself letting it all out in front of her husband and son. I decided the time was right to finally ask some of the questions I wanted to ask them.

"Do you remember the time I spent a week with you guys?"

"Of course," Bruce said.

"A little. I just remember you visiting with baby Ella," Sawyer answered.

I had forgotten Sawyer had barely been a teenager at the time, but I was referring to the summer that I gave birth to my daughter. I was having postpartum anxiety. My mom helped me as best as she could—missing work after receiving a phone call from me once a day—but we were both exhausted. I just remember Becki saying, "Come down here with Ella. Have your mom meet me halfway in Rochester. We can plan on a week for now. It might help to get away for a bit."

I trusted Becki and decided to make the trip to Iowa to see her and her family. Out of all people, I knew Becki would understand my anxiety and might be able to help. She took me in and made sure I was comfortable. She brought me to her chiropractor—her "witch doctor" as I called him. Her generosity was just her typical personality; it reminded me of the times she would treat me like one of her own daughters by buying me new clothes whenever I visited.

I had a hard time sleeping at night, though. That's when my anxiety would peak into insomnia, and hearing Ella cry made it worse. One of the nights, Becki stopped me from getting up to take care of Ella and said, "Lie down. Bruce will stay up with Ella." She crawled into bed with me and rubbed my hair, trying to calm my anxiety. She was probably rubbing my hair for a few hours total, but I still couldn't fall asleep. She even had said, "I wish I had a rubber hammer right now. I would knock you out." We just giggled. That's when she decided to take me to the emergency department of the hospital to get something for the insomnia. Becki continued to comfort me that week by those hair rubs, running me a hot bath, or her late-night runs to the gas station to get me a chicken sandwich, as I wasn't eating at all. She wanted me to take care of myself before I went back to taking care of Ella.

I needed to tell Bruce and Sawyer how much that time

meant to me because I don't think I ever had the chance to before that wedding. I always worried about how they were dealing with Becki's death, but I couldn't forget that I had my own grief as well that I never expressed. The year of my brother's wedding opened up those memories again because I found myself at another loss and my anxiety coming back when Ella experienced her own health scare with a diagnosis of Anorexia.

I expressed my worry about my own daughter to Bruce and Sawyer that night. I was afraid that I had done something wrong or there was something I could have done to prevent her condition. I wished that I had Becki's strength to stay positive through anything and thought it was unfair that she wasn't here with us anymore. I know she would have told us to come down for a week again just as she did when Ella was an infant. In that shed with my sister, Bruce, and Sawyer, they were trying to help me find the strength I needed. I knew that Ella needed a Becki of her own to help her through her treatment and be the comfort that would be by her side through the night.

We are fortunate that Ella has made a recovery since then. Surprisingly, she has become *my* strength. During her recovery, she asked if she could be baptized. Watching her choose her own path of strengthening was a proud moment as a mother. I found comfort through her baptism and through Psalm 46:5 (NIV), which states, "God is within her; she will not fall."[1] From that day, she has worn a cross as a necklace. Even through tears of the times classmates ridicule or question her choice to be faithful, she has continued to wear her cross and continues to inspire me with her bravery. I believe that I've become more faithful myself through her. We even sing along to the local Christian station in the car and still pray for our blessings every night.

There are many times that I still think of Becki. If I need

to cry out loud to myself, I listen to *Becki's Songs*, the CD that was played at her wake service. I then break out in a laugh because "Rehab"[2] by Amy Winehouse plays next. Often, my family tells me, "Wow, that was such an Aunt Becki thing to say/do!" I just think, "I hope I can be as good of a person as her."

The memory of her helping me in my time of need after Ella's birth will always be special for me. Ella is that reminder that Becki's strength is still present—as well as her personality. Even at Becki's funeral, when the whole church was eerily quiet, Ella proved how much she was like her great-aunt by farting on the hardwood pew—breaking the silence. I wanted to laugh, but I saw some of my family embarrassed and angry at my toddler's innocence. Looking at that memory now, I don't want to hold back the laughter. Becki would have done the exact same thing. We needed that laugh at the funeral and the reminder that strength can come from those whimsical moments. Strength comes from the positive memories and the wisdom she gave us about life and relationships.

Ten years later, I am now engaged to be married to my soul mate, my best friend. Someone who I've not just settled on but my knight in shining armor, my happy ending. My big day will, of course, be missing Becki, but I feel her presence and I know she will make some silly sign that she is with us. Please Becki—nothing too embarrassing.

11 "Every Breath You Take"

The hardest part about finding strength through grief is learning how to breathe again.

Strength; a word in conjunction with power, might, force, and energy. Coming from Germanic origins, one definition reads "the capacity of an object or substance to withstand great force or pressure."[1] In honesty, this definition holds a physical connotation that I've never felt I've been able to uphold. My physical stature has been very reflective of my last name, leaving me the brunt of jokes growing up that may have never bothered me, but still reiterated the fact that I was weak. That's why I choose to view strength for its emotional meaning. By exhibiting or learning mental qualities that help you deal with difficult situations or events, you show your emotional strength.

Our society uses the phrase "stay strong" frequently when tragedies occur. Little boys are often told to "man up!" or are discouraged from showing emotions in order to present a strong front. Even if we don't fully mean it, we are portraying the message that showing emotions is not human, that if we are able to hold in the tears, we are a mental warrior. Not to mention, in recent culture, the labels of "overly sensitive" or "precious snowflake" are used when we express our emotions or viewpoints too frequently (or more than the listener would like to hear). We walk a fine line in between two extremes: leaning more toward this acceptable, robotic behavior or toward being the caring individuals our biological nature has meant us to be.

I am fortunate to have had two parents who encouraged strength through emotions. I've embraced the feminine and empathic nature that my mom has given and shown me, and I've admired my dad for his willingness to show emotion in front of us kids. I will always remember the times that my dad has teared up around me, such as when the song "I Swear" was played at her wake and at various milestones in my life. He taught me that showing grief was acceptable. He was a contributing factor in how I was able to trust others with my emotional baggage and finally vocalize my story.

I have no doubt had a long road in the story thus far. In that time, I've been able to put my own grief into perspective. Drew's death opened my eyes to a different and unexpected form of grief that I had not experienced yet, but it also further put into perspective that many other people experienced that loss than just me. I know my side of the narrative and have found the ability to express it in numerous ways, helping me to feel stronger than my grief. Yet every grief is different—unexpected, expected, ambiguous loss, loss of various roles in the family, divorce, and so on. Every story is different. What if we took the time to listen to more of these stories? What if we gave people the opportunity they so desperately need to share their grief? While other people are finding their strength through vocalizing their grief, would we also find more strength in ourselves by listening?

Fast-forward to about a year after Drew's death, I was graduating from college. I was about to begin another chapter in my life and this time, I didn't have the daily structure of schooling to provide my motivation. I now had to find the internal motivation and strength to ready myself for my adult career. In a seemingly counterproductive move, my first decision was to take a break that following fall season once I had completed one last summer tour with the mission-trip company that provided me the weekly public speaking opportunities. I had no plans except a six-month internship that was set to start that following January; the last clinical experience I needed to be able to take my clinical boards as a music therapist.

"But what are you going to do until then?" my dad asked after I arrived home from my tour.

Self-care and self-discovery. That was the answer I wanted to say to everyone who asked me similar questions. For once, I was going to give myself a blank schedule to reset my body's physical and psychological clocks. Instead of following a prescribed pattern of moving on to one thing after the next, I froze time. By this time, I had seen numerous losses, traveled close to every state in the United States, and met many amazing people along the way. I felt no shame in slowing my pace for a couple of months. I wasn't taking a step back; instead, I was mentally going back in time to gain more strength from the family, friends, and community that kept me on this journey.

For that, I was lucky enough to live with my dad in my childhood home during that fall break. This gave me the ability to visit my grandmother more, visit Sydney and her beautiful and growing family, and be able to hold Mallory's second child shortly after he was born. Considering I didn't know where life would take me after my internship, this family time was crucial for me. Had I decided to start my last lap of clinical training right away, I would have missed these opportunites and missed another important moment at my cousin Adam's wedding:

"Do you remember the time I spent a week with you guys?" my cousin Meghan asked my dad and me in my aunt Terri's small chicken shed. The story that poured from her heart astounded me as she described her vivid memories of my mom providing her comfort and strength in some of her roughest moments. My cousin had held this grief in for so long and had found herself in another challenging road in her life, searching for strength for herself and for her daughter. I began to wonder if there were more stories being held at bay by my mom's family and friends.

In that following month, this curiosity was pulled in further. I had taken a role as a substitute for the paraprofessionals in my hometown's elementary and middle schools, the same role my mother had put her heart into. Working in my old elementary school with many of the same teachers who helped raise me was humbling, but it also empowered me each day when her old coworkers shared their own stories of my mom.

"Becki and I were both in the preschool special education classroom when we worked together. It was so hard moving here from my hometown and dealing with that change, but she helped me feel at home. She was my vent, laughing partner, shopping partner, and above all else, best friend," the school's nurse assistant, Lori, had shared. I had always known her as one of my mom's closest friends, but never knew their origin story. As I worked with her each day, I would get more of her side of the narrative until she shared with me a piece of information I had not known.

"I held Becki's hand as she took her last breath. Oh, how I miss my friend so much!" Lori said, providing another heartfelt reminiscence. Through her sharing, I found myself considering another perspective I had not thought of—I hadn't actually witnessed her final moments, but others had. Maybe I was lucky I didn't have to experience those last few breaths, but many stronger individuals weren't as lucky; they had to endure that moment. Lori had lost a friend the same day I'd lost my mother, and although we'd lost the same person, our losses couldn't be compared. The depth and relationship to the loss can only be understood and expressed by the one who experienced the loss.

Therefore, Meghan and Lori were just the beginning. No matter where I went, one of her friends, colleagues, or my other family members were ready and willing to offer me more stories into my mom's life. I was older, and I was grasping for a more complete picture of this woman besides the memories I'd observed through a child's and teenager's view. I wanted to know how grief had affected those close to her.

"I remember the last time I talked to her. I gave her a call to see how she was doing. She told me she wasn't feeling very well, and she was waiting to hear back from her doctor," another one of my mom's friends, Deb, stated as she gave me a haircut one day. "As we were ready to quit talking, I told her to take care. I told her how much she meant to me, how much I loved her, and that I cherished our friendship. She said the same to me. I think we both knew it would be the last time we would speak to each other. The next day, she died."

Deb had cut my hair for most of my life and many of my memories of getting those haircuts revolved around my mom smiling and laughing in the corner of the room as her and her dear friend took those times to chat. Deb expressed grief over not being at the hospital that day, but as she described, "I was very glad to have had the opportunity to fix Becki's hair for her funeral. I wondered if it would be emotionally difficult to do it, but honestly, I felt quite at peace and happy doing it. It was as if I had one last chance to be with her. I could talk to her, tell her goodbye privately and do her hair one last time. One last thing I could do for my dear friend."

"Being a nurse during that time was the worst thing I thought I could be, as I knew what was in store for my sister and family," my aunt Laura shared. She continued:

> Becki asked our cousin, Kay, and me to go with her to her consultation with the oncologist to help her understand the medical lingo and help decide what was going to be the best treatment course for her cancer. She told the doctor that she didn't want anyone giving her a time line or time frame for when she was going to die, and adamantly told the doctor that she wanted both Kay and me to look at the CAT scan results.
>
> As I read them, I swallowed hard to chase the tears from my face and voice. I didn't want to cry in front of her as she was being so strong. The doctors were going to examine her, and so Bruce, Kay, and I left the room. As soon as we got into the waiting room, all three of us sobbed. A lot of heartache was let loose on each other's shoulders. I was going to lose my best friend, and it wasn't a matter of if, but when. I felt like I was being crushed in a vice.
>
> When she died, the emptiness couldn't compare. I had lost my brother many years prior and felt that loss, but not like my friend and confidante—Becki. I saw my dad lose the lust for life that once kept him from dying from his severe stroke. He slowly deteriorated as the light went out of his soul. He maintained long enough to help my mom emotionally get through

> her cancer and was finally so tired that he was falling all the time and needed to be placed in a nursing home.
>
> I believe that her death made me choose to switch what kind of nursing that I did. I waited for a place to open a hospice position for me as an LPN and I was finally given that opportunity in Cedar Rapids in 2016, allowing me to move back to Iowa. I feel like this is what she would have wanted me to do. I now help both patients and their families journey toward the end of life here on earth, and I know that there is a place called heaven waiting for them and us.

All of these years, my sisters and I had been ruminating on the fact that as the children in this story, we weren't told the full extent of her disease. In light of my aunt's perspective, I understand now that knowing too much can cause just as much pain as not knowing enough. My aunt Laura watched my mom's decline through a medical lens and had to accept reality before many of us did. Life as a nurse made grief hit close to home.

What about far from home, though? What is grief like for those friends separated by many miles between them? Linda Craig, her roommate and friend from when she went to school in California, gave insight on this long-distance grief:

> Even after she moved back to Iowa, our many miles apart didn't matter; our bond was strong. We kept in touch through numerous phone calls: her sharing the news of her first child and me calling her, asking her to be my maid of honor. She was excited when I was next to call about the news that I was pregnant with twins, offering me advice and blessings. She was

equally as supportive and loving when I called eighteen weeks later with the news that I had a miscarriage.

When I became pregnant again, she was who I called when my husband and I learned that our baby boy was diagnosed with spina bifida. I withdrew from so many friends, but Becki sent pictures of her daughter and sent gifts—always reaching out to me to help me with my inner fear of the unknown. Robert, our son, was born, and life was beautiful with our baby boy. It was also different than others, but this was all we knew. Finally, when our daughter, Morgan, was born, Becki and Bruce became the obvious choice for her godparents, a call Becki happily accepted. As life got more hectic, our calls were months apart; however, when I heard her voice, it felt like it was yesterday.

But, one day the call was different. The home phone rang, and my husband, Bob, came to me and said: 'It's Becki.' Her tone was very solemn, and she shared the news of what she had been dealing with—her fears. I hung up the phone, and Bob had already looked up flights and wanted to know when I wanted to go visit her. This trip was so important to me. It was going to be a long goodbye, face to face.

When I visited, I loved meeting her friends and seeing her beautiful family all grown up, but I was struck by a large plaque hanging in her kitchen with the phrase: **Life is not measured by the number of breaths we take, but by the moments that take our breath away.**

Within that visit, Becki and I had our final conversation. One of the most amazing

> conversations that I will cherish until I take my last breath.

My own breath was being taken away, crying tears of joy as I found how others' words were filling me back up. It appeared that my mom had helped others through grief of their own. It also appeared that somehow these individuals were strong enough to be with her, knowing it would be their last interaction. Taking the time to listen to others' experiences with grief was showing me the various ways and viewpoints that have helped people cope.

I had briefly had an experience with this story sharing in school when my high school had offered a grief group for students who had experienced a death in their life. I only remembered attending twice—getting to miss class—but I remember wanting to be with these other students. Although nothing we talked about was groundbreaking, I enjoyed knowing that other people had similar, yet vastly different, experiences with grief. I found a glimmer of strength from learning these different perspectives. There was strength in numbers.

Thus, I did what I should have done a lot sooner in this ten-year journey—I personally asked my own family to provide their full stories. I began to ask the question: In your perspective, what was the hardest part about losing her? The perspective chapters in this book were born from these interviews and the personal writings of the family and friends of my mom—providing a more complete picture and showing the strength that we have gained through the years. We all had to learn something about ourselves while facing a different side of grief, and we all had to find our way through the reconstitution and resolution of grief in order to build our resilience for future grief; but how did we do that?

Reconstitution, a term for the postdeath period, describes

the changing views of one's self and views of the relationships with those surrounding the death.[2] I began to notice similarities in how each perspective worked through the reconstitution period; accepting the reality that she had died, experiencing the pain of the loss, adjusting to life without her, and maintaining a meaningful connection with her as we reinvested in other relationships. These are all necessary tasks, as described by J. William Worden, that can help lead to grief resolution.[3] Of these tasks, retaining a meaningful bond with my mom as we moved forward with our lives and with other relationships helped my family the most.

I had done just that—strengthening my relationship with friends after my first anxiety attack. Similarly, both of my sisters deepened their relationship with their boyfriends, which led to their eventual marriages. The greatest example of moving forward with other relationships, however, lies within my dad's story. With my mom's blessing, he continued his life with someone else, while keeping her memory alive. He accepted the fact that someone had to die first within the marriage and as C. S. Lewis put it, bereavement is simply "one of [marriage's] regular phases—like the honeymoon."[4]

I'll admit that I sometimes worry about the fact that both my father and his father lost a wife prematurely on the same date—April 10. Does this mean I am next to lose a wife to a terminal illness on this spring date? The odds are doubtful, but I at least know that my dad's ability to make room for someone new is an example that reconstitution is possible in widowhood.

Within another framework of resolution, Tedeschi and Calhoun describe additional forms of post-traumatic growth: finding personal strength, seeing new possibilities, discovering more meaning in life, and gaining appreciation.[5] We had all found personal strength in ourselves when we stepped back into our daily lives after her funeral. That personal strength was also described through Meghan's and my vocalization of our stories to other people. However, my aunt LeAnne's story of seeking counseling, changing her career, and accepting her own identity required her to understand what her personal strength was. She sought new possibilities in her career and used my mother's everlasting support to guide her to a new happiness.

The path to discovering more meaning in life was also present in each of our perspectives. I may have started with seeking meaning of smaller things, such as my gut feelings, the storms, and the butterflies, but I found greater meaning in my own life through my relationship to music and faith. This quest for meaning ultimately led to my career as a music therapist. Within my sisters' stories, both of them were compelled to fulfill their own meaningful roles as mothers. The growth they have described within themselves is reflective of the impact my mom had on them, even leading both of them to incorporate the letter Y into the names of their first child; a unique tradition my mom subtly started. I came to this conclusion very late in life, but after my mom changed the spelling of her name from Becky to Becki in order to distinguish her name from her cousin's wife (of the same first and last name), she incorporated a Y into each of her children's names—including her puppy child, Pyper. I guess even my mom had a meaning for everything.

Finding meaning in her death finally brought us to appreciation—a humbling form of post-traumatic growth and resolution. Each author in my mom's story chronicled the appreciation gained after accepting and identifying the changes her death brought. Mallory wrote of her appreciation toward my mom's strength for being able to leave us children, knowing that us kids were in good hands. Like my own realization when listening to Dance Marathon families speak of losing their child to cancer, Mallory understood that we were lucky to have had our mother for as long as we did. There are grief stories that are not as fortunate enough to have had as much time. There are parents, such as my grandmother, who experience the additional grief and guilt of living longer than their children.

The greatest form of appreciation to come from all of these perspectives is the sense of family. I came to this hard realization when I missed out on family members' milestones and was more worried about myself. Developmentally, I was normal for wanting to have greater independence and establish intimate relationships outside of my family, but this only presented a struggle as I tried to balance these desires with the needs of my family. I was, thus, mourning my mom as the family organizer and my adviser.[6] Sydney had commented on her own "self-absorbed" personality and expressed her own guilt for not coming back home to help my dad raise me. We all yearned for my mom, "the nucleus of the family," as my aunt LeAnne had succinctly stated.

In her death, we had to learn how to form our own nucleus. We had to find a way to come together on our own and take on the strength that she had, a strength that was finally tested after I graduated college.

"Sawyer, Grandpa Wagner is having a hard time breathing. They believe he's in his last few days," my dad said on the phone. I was on the last week of my mission-trip tour and hoping within that moment that my grandpa could last long enough for me to arrive home. Regardless, I made the video call to my grandma and soon realized that most of my extended family were already present within his nursing home room. I was tearing up; strength was in numbers. I was able to say my last words to my grandpa—the man who taught strength to my mother and to our family. He wasn't able to verbally respond, but my grandma said, "He heard you. He just squeezed my hand as you spoke!"

My grandpa passed away that next morning, exactly a year after Drew's death. I like to believe that this wasn't a coincidence as both of these men had taught me how to be strong. My grandpa showed me how to build and value a strong family, while Drew helped build up my emotional strength, supporting me even in those small moments such as when I briefly lost my "Livestrong" bracelet. They deserved to share the same day.

A sense of relief had overcome me, just as I had experienced when Pyper had died and just as LeAnne had stated when she received the call that Becki had died; they were no longer suffering. My grandmother was no longer having to struggle being both a spouse and caretaker for her husband. Even in the midst of the sadness, relief can and should be expressed. As Kubler-Ross and Kessler stated, relief "is not disloyalty but rather a sign of deep love."[7] Relief took the place of this long-awaited anticipation that we all had felt since the stroke my grandpa had experienced eleven years prior.

My cousin Adam's wedding that following month was a coming together of our family beyond the funeral. I once again saw our extended family enjoying each other's presences. I witnessed expression of grief and a cousin's vulnerability incongruously juxtaposed with the comical setting of a chicken shed. I simply witnessed our family being a family again. I knew then that somehow we had moved through our periods of reconstitution and found somewhat of a resolution. We had let go of the guilt and the prohibition of emotions that were holding us from resolving our grief.[8] We had found emotional rest in each other and had found strength within our periods of weakness.

As stated in 2 Corinthians 12:10 (NLT), "That's why I take pleasure in my weaknesses, and in the insults, hardships, persecutions, and troubles that I suffer for Christ. For when I am weak, then I am strong."[9]

We may feel out of breath in our periods of weakness. When enduring the pain of running a marathon, you are presented with many moments that take your breath away; but, in order for muscles to grow and for yourself to get stronger, you must go through these challenges and experience the weakness. The trials build your resilience and leave you with lasting memories. As my mom's friend Linda was writing her side of the story and allowing herself to reexperience her own moments of weakness, she stated:

"I was driving my son, Rob, to a doctor's appointment. I was telling him how much I missed Becki and how difficult it was to complete these thoughts because it was so emotional. As we were driving down the freeway, I noticed that the song on the radio was the tune from the song, 'Every Breath You Take,' but the words were different. I turned up the radio, and it was Puff Daddy's remix, 'I'll Be Missing You.' I know this was Becki's sign."

Every step I take, every move I make (I miss you)
Every single day, every time I pray,
I'll be missing you
Thinkin' of the day when you went away
What a life to take, what a bond to break
I'll be missin' you[10]

There are many moments in your life that will take your breath away. So with every breath you take, let it give you strength.

Conclusion: "May the Road Rise to Meet You"

After all these years, I am willing and able to add to my family's compilation of grief reflections by providing my own statement about our butterfly:

> **The hardest part about losing a mother is knowing that I was growing up and developing my independence without my biggest supporter.**

The great thing about putting that statement out there finally is knowing that I wasn't truly alone throughout this past decade; I had that support all along. There's no doubt I am a different person because of this journey and grief transformed me. I know that wisdom can naturally come with the years, but I believe the trials and experiences were meant to give me a better outlook on life. As my mom once told me, "The world we live in can be viewed as a metaphorical Hades. If you are able to survive and find the positives within it, you will have found your heaven."

Writing this book was a daunting task to try to organize and make sense of all that occurred within a decade. I laugh at myself for thinking death would ever fully make sense, but somehow, we've got to find our meaning within the messiness. I chose to take on this task because the world needs more comforting stories and my family needed the reassurance that death is not the end of a life. There is nothing wrong with wanting to think about the deceased. If we didn't, those memories could further fade, and the person would die a second time: "a bereavement worse than the first."[1] Writing has been a cleansing for me and a look forward to growing in another decade's time.

One in nine Americans will lose a parent, and one in seven will lose a parent *or* sibling before the age of twenty.[2] Despite this fact, I and the more than 1.9 million other children in similar situations today go on and learn how to adjust.[3] Journaling, songwriting, and sharing stories through whatever means necessary has allowed me to feel connected to a bigger purpose and enabled me to process these memories. I feel more connected to my mom, and I'm proud of the characteristics that I share with her; the lessons she taught me were further amplified in importance through the process. Interestingly, discussion of stories can help children build self-esteem, and by allowing different perspectives to come together into a coherent story, children can build senses of control.[4] After this writing experience, I feel more connected to the family that I often distanced myself from when trying to prove my independence. All along, they were having similar issues in expressing this lack of connection.

The stories in this book are not the only. I would have loved to include more stories from each person who my mom had impacted. I would have loved to incorporate more stories from the families and friends of the other losses in my life as well. A whole additional book could have been written with these other stories, but in the end, I didn't want to overwhelm myself or the readers with even more unpacking of emotions. What we learn from a grief journey is that there are many secondary losses that are impacted due to the primary loss. Whether you are watching a dream die, graduating, leaving home, changing jobs, or welcoming new joys into your life—the change can trigger similar grief symptoms.

For those reading that are currently struggling through grief: know what is normal for yourself and know when it's too much. Common symptoms of grief may include fatigue, nausea, weight loss or gain, aches and pains, and insomnia. When grief grabs you, you may go through periods of anxiety, anger, loneliness, depression, and crying spells.[5] Also know that the five stages of grief (denial, anger, bargaining, depression, acceptance) as defined by Elisabeth Kubler-Ross are not meant to be all-inclusive for the emotions you may experience. Kubler-Ross herself stated that "they were never meant to help tuck messy emotions into neat packages."[6] Your grief is your own, and you may go through more or less of these stages in your own order.

Be aware of when you have crossed over to a maladaptive form of grieving. Experiencing denial or problems accepting the death, having feelings of numbness and detachment, feeling like life is empty, and being stuck in an intense state of mourning that disrupts your daily living all may indicate that you are suffering from complicated grieving—especially if these feelings persist after a year has passed. At this point, you should consider seeking professional help. Websites, such as from the Mayo Clinic and various others, are included at the end of this book for more information on complicated grief. Not to mention, social media sites may help lead you to online support groups or memorial pages for the loved one that passed away, allowing you and others to share your stories.

As for my own grief, it has been repackaged yet again through this writing process. Where I last checked my grief, it was held within a beautiful and bright flower. Today and forever, I view my grief in the two bracelets I still have on my wrist: Jana's "Livestrong" bracelet that has withstood trials in the years since she gave it to me, and a newer blue bracelet that shines as a memorial for Drew—simply stating, "Fly High, Drew." The great thing about these grief containers is that they don't weigh me down. I don't have to carry them with me wherever I go. Instead, they are attached to me—a part of me—and they allow me to acknowledge them on my own time, giving me joy from all of the positive memories.

Even my mom's dedication song to us kids has been reorganized in its meaning for me through this writing experience. I typically only listen to the song on her anniversary, and so I spent most of my writing process without the presence of the full lyrics. Lyrics that implore us to not overlook the power of faith. Lyrics that encourage making those worthwhile mistakes in love. Lyrics that remind us to not take for granted the life we currently have and each breath that we take because "who wants to look back on their years and wonder where those years have gone?"[7] Whether by a subconscious effort or a destined plan, this book and my grief journey naturally became an extension of the story within her dedication song. She was continuing to give us life lessons even in death.

My mom continues to send me the butterflies, reminders that there is a lot to be thankful for. I view them as her watching over me and the butterflies cause me to reminisce of a time when my mom had discussed this same viewpoint: "I don't know who your guardian angel is, but whoever they are, better know I'm coming for their job." My belief in a guardian angel is further proof that religion and spirituality has given me hope and comfort. Through the trauma, I found growth and resilience in part because of faith.[8]

I like the idea of things becoming full circle—that there is a reason for the suffering. I am where I need to be and am able to find the why in every situation. No matter where I go and no matter what happens, the road will rise to meet me.

As stated in James 1:2–4 (NLT): "Dear brothers and sisters, when troubles of any kind come your way, consider it an opportunity for great joy. For you know that when your faith is tested, your endurance has a chance to grow. So let it grow, for when your endurance is fully developed, you will be perfect and complete, needing nothing."[9]

Faith can provide the grounding you need in periods of grief. However, seek what allows you to express your emotions to its fullest. I have a bias toward music, but that's due to the numerous ways music neurologically can help provide relief. When trauma shuts down the expressive speech portion of your brain's left hemisphere, leaving you at a loss for words, music reception—which comes from the right hemisphere—can help nonverbally communicate those emotions and help lead to resolution.[10] Whether you are creating or recording memorial CDs for yourself or with the dying individual, writing songs about the memories you have, or simply listening to songs associated with the death, music can be your solace.

During my last visit home before I made my move from Iowa to Nashville, Tennessee, to begin my career as a music therapist, I pulled out my copy of *Becki's Songs* and was taken on a musical journey through her diagnosis and death. I knew at that moment that I wanted to start writing this book, but I didn't know where to begin. There was too much to unpack, and I couldn't put the pen to paper—or fingers to keyboard, I suppose. I thought, The hardest part about reflecting on my grief journey is finding the right words to start the story. Thus, I spent most of my time sifting through my mom's old stuff to get ideas.

That's when I stumbled upon a familiar journal with a three-dimensional tree design on it. I untied the leather string from the front cover and opened it up to find that loose piece of paper inserted in the book. I smiled at the familiar handwriting and funeral plans that helped guide my journey. I flipped through the journal pages, wondering if I could use it to write my book in, and I soon realized that I had overlooked a page all of these years.

It appeared my mom did in fact write in this journal! She had already started her own story but didn't get far; her story was unfinished. On the very first page, she had written a few words; an incomplete sentence that I could start with. The rest we all would complete.

One of the hardest things
about b

NOTES

Introduction

1 Van der Kolk, 1998, S52–S54 about research on trauma and memories.
2 Roiphe, 2008.
3 Children survivors. Social Security Administration, "Benefits Paid by Type of Beneficiary," accessed on March 10, 2018: www.ssa.gov/oact/progdata/icp.html.
4 Bright, 2002, especially introduction chapter for an expansive list of types of losses.
5 Bright, 2002, chapter 4 for discussion on the extent of emotional pain with bereavement.
6 Song by Lonestar. Derry and Diamond, 2002.
7 McGaugh, 2013, for further study of memory and emotion.
8 Bremner, 2006, for further study of neural plasticity and effects of traumatic stress.
9 Bartlett, 2003, for further discussion on memory and the theory of schema.
10 John Hinton, *Dying* (Pelican, 1967).
11 Hood, 2009, chapter three for full context of quote.

Chapter 1: Newly Diagnosed Teenager

1 Mayo Clinic, 2017, for full article on anemia symptoms and causes.

Chapter 3: The Butterfly Effect

1 Jung 1963, 340 for quote and further exploration of the psyche.
2 Song by All-4-One, a cover of John Michael Montgomery's single. Baker and Myers, 1994.
3 Song by Lee Ann Womack. Sillers and Sanders, 1999.
4 Rosen and Tesser, 1970, for further discussion of the mum effect.

Perspective: The Sister

1 Weight Watchers: www.weightwatchers.com for more information on the program.

Chapter 4: High School (the) Musical

1 Bright, 2002, 99.
2 Bright, 2002, 99 for full quote.
3 Livestrong bracelet. www.livestrong.org for more information: a foundation that provides services to those affected by cancer.

Chapter 5: "We Are Family, I've Got All My Baggage with Me"

1 Rowling, 1997 – 2007.
2 Song by Three Dog Night. Newman, 1970.
3 Song by Mariah Carey. Carey, et. al., 1996.
4 Song by Sister Sledge. Edwards and Rodgers, 1979.
5 Nouwen, 1990, for full quote.
6 Song by The CO. The CO, 2010.
7 Scene from the sixth film in the Harry Potter series. *Harry Potter and the Half-Blood Prince*, 2009.

Chapter 6: "Waiting on the World to Change"

1 Boss, 2000, for a thorough description of the potential causes and reactions to ambiguous loss.
2 Lewis, 1994, 62 (chapter 4).

3 American Music Therapy Association website: musictherapy.org for more information on music therapy as a profession.
4 Catholic Heart Workcamp website: heartworkcamp.com for more information on the organization's mission.

Chapter 7: "All You Need Is Love"

1 Nunn, et. al., 2000, for the memory capabilities of various brain regions and structures.
2 McGaugh, et al., 1996, for the involvement of amygdala on memory storage.
3 Song by Britney Spears. Dennis, et. al., 2004.
4 Tomaino, 2015, for more on music's effects on the brain.
5 Film by DreamWorks. "Shrek," 2001.
6 Foa and Meadows, 1997, for discussion on traumatic stress.
7 Walton, 1996, 89 (Chapter 17).
8 "All We Said," an original song by Sawyer Small, 2011.

Chapter 8: "In the Cycle, the Cycles of Life"

1 Kubler-Ross and Kessler, 2014, especially chapter 1 for discussion on the depression stage of grief.
2 Sandberg and Grant, 2017, introduction chapter for full quote.
3 Boy Scouts of America website: scouting.org for more information on requirements of an Eagle Scout.
4 "With You," an original song by Sawyer Small, 2012.

Chapter 9: "I Hope You Dance"

1 Children's Miracle Network Hospitals—Dance Marathon website for: information on the movement, a local program near you, and how to donate.
2 Christ, 2002, 1277, & Sandberg and Grant, 2017, p. 68, for the positive effects of active contributions on reducing feelings of hopelessness and building resilience in bereavement.
3 Facebook Page: Cally's Cause—The Chemo Bag, for more information on how to donate and receive services for a loved one.

4 Feldman and Kravetz, 2015, for further discussion on grounded hope.
5 Lyrics from Sillers and Sanders, 1999.

Chapter 10: "Edelweiss"

1 Lewis, 1994.
2 Kubler-Ross and Kessler, 2014, 62–63, for discussion on the inner world of grief: the story.
3 *The Bible.* New Living Translation Version, 2015, Philippians 4:13.
4 Quick, 1956. Choral arrangement.
5 Singh, 1996. Choral arrangement.
6 Traditional Irish blessing: "May the road rise to meet you. May the wind be always at your back. May the sun shine warm upon your face, the rains fall soft upon your fields, and until we meet again, may God hold you in the palm of his hand."
7 Show tune from *The Sound of Music.* Rodgers & Hammerstein, 1959.

Perspective: The Niece/Goddaughter

1 *The Bible.* New International Version, 2011, Psalm 46:5.
2 Song by Amy Winehouse. Winehouse, 2006.

Chapter 11: "Every Breath You Take"

1 To Merriam Webster Online Dictionary.
2 Christ, 2000, for full definition of reconstitution, as opposed to the term, recovery.
3 Worden, 1991, for further discussion on the necessary tasks for resolution.
4 Lewis, 1994, for full quote in the foreword.
5 Tedeschi and Calhoun, 1996, for a full discussion of the various forms of post-traumatic growth.
6 Christ, 2002, for the developmental needs of the various ages of grieving children and adolescents.

7 Kubler-Ross and Kessler's, 2014, especially chapter 2 for full quote and discussion of relief after a death.
8 Bright, 2002, introductory chapter for discussion of the obstacles of grief resolution, especially matters that originate in the attitudes of others.
9 *The Bible.* New Living Translation Version, 2015, 2 Corinthians 12:10.
10 Song by Puff Daddy and Faith Evans. Evans, et. al., 1997.

Conclusion: "May the Road Rise to Meet You"

1 Lewis, 1994, for full quote in chapter 4.
2 Comfort Zone reference: poll of 1,006 adults conducted via the internet November 24–December 7, 2009 by national polling firm of Matthew Greenwald & Associate, Inc.
3 Social Security Administration, "Benefits Paid by Type of Beneficiary."
4 Fivush, et. al., 2004, for further discussion on children's emotional well-being through family narratives.
5 Mayo Clinic articles, "Complicated Grief," 2017, and "Grief: Coping with Reminders after a Loss," 2015, for more information on grief support.
6 Kubler-Ross and Kessler, 2014, for full quote in the foreword to the anniversary edition.
7 Sillers and Sanders, 1999.
8 Shaw, et. al., 2005, for further discussion on the impact religion and spirituality have on posttraumatic growth.
9 *The Bible.* New Living Translation Version, 2015, James 1:2–4.
10 Van der Kolk, 1998, S52 – S54.

BIBLIOGRAPHY

"About Music Therapy & AMTA." *American Music Therapy Association*, www.musictherapy.org.

"About Us." *Catholic Heart Workcamp,* www.heartworkcamp.com.

"Anemia." *Mayo Clinic*, Mayo Foundation for Medical Education and Research, 8 Aug. 2017, www.mayoclinic.org/diseases-conditions/anemia/symptoms-causes/syc-20351360.

Baker, Gary and Frank J. Myers. "All-4-One." *I Swear,* Apr. 1994.

Balk, David E., and Charles A. Corr. "Bereavement During Adolescence." *Handbook of Bereavement Research,* edited by Margaret S. Stroebe, et al., Washington, DC, American Psychological Association, 2001, 199–218.

Bartlett, Frederic C. *Remembering: A Study in Experimental and Social Psychology.* Cambridge University Press, 1932.

Boss, Pauline. *Ambiguous Loss: Learning to Live with Unresolved Grief.* Harvard University Press, 2000.

"Boy Scouting." *Boy Scouts of America*, www.scouting.org/programs/boy-scouts/.

Bremner, J. Douglas. "Traumatic Stress: Effects on the Brain." *Dialogues in Clinical Neuroscience*, vol. 8, no. 4, 2006, 445–461.

Bright, Ruth. *Supportive Eclectic Music Therapy for Grief and Loss: A Practical Handbook for Professionals.* MMB Music, 2002.

Carey, Mariah, et al. "Daydream." *Always Be My Baby*, Mar. 1996.

Christ, Grace Hyslop., et al. "Adolescent Grief: It Never Really Hit Me ... Until It Actually Happened." *Jama*, vol. 288, no. 10, Nov. 2002, 1269–1278.

Christ, Grace Hyslop. *Healing Children's Grief: Surviving a Parent's Death from Cancer.* Oxford University Press, 2000.

"Complicated Grief." *Mayo Clinic*, Mayo Foundation for Medical Education and Research, 5 Oct. 2017, www.mayoclinic.org/diseases-conditions/complicated-grief/symptoms-causes/syc-20360374.

"Dance Marathon." *Children's Miracle Network*, https://dancemarathon.childrensmiraclenetworkhospitals.org.

Dennis, Cathy, et. al. "In the Zone." *Toxic*, Jan. 2004.

Derry, Maribeth, and Steve Diamond. "I'm Already There." *Not a Day Goes By*, Jan. 2002.

"Dictionary by Merriam-Webster: America's Most-Trusted Online Dictionary." *Merriam-Webster*, Merriam-Webster, www.merriam-webster.com.

Edwards, Bernard and Nile Rodgers. "We Are Family." *We Are Family*, Apr. 1979.

Evans, Faith, et. al. "No Way Out." *I'll Be Missing You*, May 1997.

Feldman, David B., and Lee Daniel Kravetz. *Supersurvivors: the Surprising Link between Suffering and Success.* Harperwave, an Imprint of HarperCollinsPublishers, 2015.

Fivush, Robyn, et. al. "Family Narratives and the Development of Children's Emotional Well-Being." *Family Stories and the Life Course Across Time and Generations*, edited by Michael W. Pratt and Barbara Fiese, Taylor and Francis, 2004.

Foa, E. B., and E. A. Meadows. "Psychosocial Treatments for Posttraumatic Stress Disorder: A Critical Review." *Annual Review of Psychology*, vol. 48, no. 1, 1997, 449–480.

"Grief: Coping with Reminders after a Loss." *Mayo Clinic*, Mayo Foundation for Medical Education and Research, 24 Sept. 2015, www.mayoclinic.org/healthy-lifestyle/end-of-life/in-depth/grief/art-20045340.

Harry Potter and the Half-Blood Prince. Warner Bros. Entertainment Inc., 2009.

Hinton, John. *Dying*. Pelican, 1967.

Hood, Ann. *Comfort: A Journey through Grief*. W.W. Norton & Co., 2009.

Jung, C. G. *Memories, Dreams, Reflections*. Pantheon Books, 1963.

Kolk, Bessel A. Van Der. "Trauma and Memory." *Psychiatry and Clinical Neurosciences*, vol. 52, no. S1, Sept. 1998, S52–S64.

Kübler-Ross, Elisabeth, and David Kessler. *On Grief & Grieving: Finding the Meaning of Grief through the Five Stages of Loss*. Simon & Schuster, 2014.

Lewis, C. S. *A Grief Observed*. HarperOne, an Imprint of HarperCollinsPublishers, 1994.

"Life with Grief Research." *Comfort Zone Camp*, July 2010, www.comfortzonecamp.org/news/childhood-bereavement-study-results.

"LIVESTRONG." *LIVESTRONG*, www.livestrong.org/.

McGaugh, James L., et al. "Involvement of the Amygdala in Memory Storage: Interaction with Other Brain

Systems." *Proceedings of the National Academy of Sciences*, vol. 93, no. 24, 1996, 13508–13514.

McGaugh, James L. "Memory and Emotion: the Making of Lasting Memories." *Proceedings of the National Academy of Sciences*, vol. 110, no. 02, 18 June 2013, 10402–10407.

Newman, Randy. "It Ain't Easy." *Mama Told Me (Not to Come)*, May 1970.

Nouwen, Henri J. M. *Out of Solitude Three Meditations on the Christian Life*. Library of Congress, NLS/BPH, 1990.

Nunn, Kenneth, et al. *Who's Who of the Brain: A Guide to Its Inhabitants, Where They Live and What They Do.* Jessica Kingsley Publishers, 2008.

Quick, Clarence E. "Come Go with Me." *Come Go with Me*, Dec. 1956.

Resick, Patricia A., and Monica K. Schnicke. "Cognitive Processing Therapy for Sexual Assault Victims." *Journal of Consulting and Clinical Psychology*, vol. 60, no. 5, 1992, 748–756.

Rodgers, Richard and Oscar Hammerstein. *The Sound of Music*. "Edelweiss." 1959.

Roiphe, Anne. *Epilogue: A Memoire*. HarperCollins Publishers, 2008.

Rosen, Sidney, and Abraham Tesser. "On Reluctance to Communicate Undesirable Information: The MUM Effect." *Sociometry,* vol. 33, no. 3, 1970, 253–263.

Rowling, J. K. Harry Potter Series. Scholastic, 1997–2007.

Sandberg, Sheryl, and Adam Grant. *Option B: Facing Adversity, Building Resilience and Finding Joy.* Alfred A. Knopf, 2017.

Shaw, Annick, et al. "Religion, Spirituality, and Posttraumatic Growth: A Systematic Review." *Mental Health, Religion & Culture*, vol. 8, no. 1, 2005, 1–11.

"Shrek." DreamWorks, 2001.

Sillers, Tia, and Mark D. Sanders. "I Hope You Dance." *I Hope You Dance*, Sept. 1999.

Sing, Vijay. *Fergus an' Molly*. Alfred Publishing Co., Inc., 1996.

"Social Security." *Types of Beneficiaries*, www.ssa.gov/OACT/ProgData/types.html.

Tedeschi, Richard G., and Lawrence G. Calhoun. "The Posttraumatic Growth Inventory: Measuring the Positive Legacy of Trauma." *Journal of Traumatic Stress*, vol. 9, no. 3, 1996, 455–471.

The Bible. New International Version. Biblica, Inc., 2011.

The Bible. New Living Translation Version. Tyndale House Publishers, 2015.

The CO. "The Co." *Keep It Together*, 2010.

Tomaino, Concetta M. "Music Therapy and the Brain." *Music Therapy Handbook*, edited by Barbara L. Wheeler, The Guilford Press, 2015, 40–50.

Walton, Charlie. *When There Are No Words: Finding Your Way to Cope with Loss and Grief*. Pathfinder, 1996.

Winehouse, Amy. "Back to Black." *Rehab*, Oct. 2006.

Worden, J. William. *Grief Counseling and Grief Therapy*. Fourth ed., Springer Publishing Company, LLC, 2008.

AVAILABLE GRIEF SUPPORT

Aiding Mothers and Fathers Experiencing Neonatal Death (AMEND)

- AMEND is a nonprofit organization that offers support and "free counseling service to parents who have experienced the loss of an infant through miscarriage, stillbirth, or neonatal death." (amendgroup.com)

American Association of Suicidology (AAS)

- Nonprofit organization that promotes "the understanding and prevention of suicide and [supports] those who have been affected by it." (suicidology.org)

American Music Therapy Association (AMTA)

- A resource and organization dedicated to professional music therapists. Benefits gained from using music as a tool include help educating, reducing stress, and improve the general quality of life. (musictherapy.org)

Cally's Cause—The Chemo Bag

- A nonprofit organization dedicated to providing hand-sewn bags filled with supplies that can help people cope with chemo treatments. See Cally's Cause—The Chemo Bag Facebook Page for information on how to donate or request a chemo bag for a loved one.

Centering Corporation

- Centering Corporation has grief resources for "infant loss, bereaved parents, suicide, homicide, loss of a spouse, children and grief, pet loss, general grief resources and more." (centering.org)

The Compassionate Friends

- A nonprofit organization that "provides highly personal comfort, hope, and support to every family experiencing the death of a son or a daughter, a brother or a sister, or a grandchild, and helps others better assist the grieving family." (compassionatefriends.org)

Dance Marathon (Children's Miracle Network Hospitals)

- A movement of over four hundred K–12 and collegiate-based programs in North America, benefitting Children's Miracle Network Hospitals. A nonprofit organization that raises funds and awareness for more than 170 pediatric hospitals across North America. (dancemarathon.childrensmiraclenetworkhospitals.org)

DivorceCare

- "A friendly, caring group of people who will walk alongside you through one of life's most difficult experiences. Don't go through separation or divorce alone." (divorcecare.org)

Dougy Center

- Center that "provides support and training locally, nationally and internationally to individuals and organizations seeking to assist children in grief." (dougy.org)

Empty Arms

- "A community resource that works to connect people with one another so that they feel less alone" after experiencing a miscarriage, stillbirth, or infant loss. (emptyarmsbereavement.org)

GriefNet

- Online support community for people dealing with grief, death, and major loss, with over fifty monitored support groups for both kids and adults. (griefnet.org)

GriefShare

- "GriefShare is a friendly, caring group of people who will walk alongside you through one of life's most difficult experiences. You don't have to go through the grieving process alone." (griefshare.org)

Hello, Grief

- "Comfort Zone Camp, Inc. developed HelloGrief.org to start a discussion about the impact of loss, and how to help grieving persons cope; as well as build a community of support for those living with grief." (hellogrief.org)

HelpGuide

- Online trusted guide to mental & emotional health. (helpguide.org)

JAMA Network

- Journal of American Medical Association: Resource for articles on mental health and grief. (jamanetwork.com)

Loving Outreach to Survivors of Suicide (LOSS)

- LOSS "is a nondenominational program that supports individuals who are grieving the loss of a loved one by suicide." (catholiccharities.net)

Mayo Clinic

- Online resource for medical advice, including symptoms of grief, complicated grief, and how to cope with complicated grief. (mayoclinic.org)

National Alliance on Mental illness (NAMI)

- NAMI "is the nation's largest grassroots mental health organization dedicated to building better lives for the millions of Americans affected by mental illness." (nami.org)

National Association of Social Workers (NASW)

- NASW is "the largest membership organization of professional social workers in the world." (socialworkers.org)

National Hospice and Palliative Care Organization

- Organization "committed to improving end-of-life care and expanding access to hospice care with the goal of profoundly enhancing quality of life for people dying in American and their loved ones." (nhpco.org)

Navigating Grief

- An educational and informational community about grief with "professional support services based on life and grief coaching practices for moving forward after loss." (navigatinggrief.com)

Parents of Murdered Children, Inc.

- An organization that provides "support and assistance to all survivors of homicide victims while working to create a world free of murder." (pomc.com)

Parents Without Partners

- PWP is "the largest international, nonprofit organization devoted to the welfare and interests of single parents and their children." (parentswithoutpartners.org)

Widowed Persons Service (AARP)

- Widowed Persons Service is an organization established by AARP and designed by people who have themselves lost a spouse in order to provide support for widows and widowers. (aarp.org)

CPSIA information can be obtained
at www.ICGtesting.com
Printed in the USA
BVHW031953061218
534856BV00028B/37/P